VIRGIL

The Aeneid

K.W. Gransden

*Reader in English and Comparative Literature,
University of Warwick*

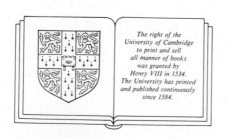

The right of the
University of Cambridge
to print and sell
all manner of books
was granted by
Henry VIII in 1534.
The University has printed
and published continuously
since 1584.

CAMBRIDGE UNIVERSITY PRESS

Cambridge

New York   Port Chester

Melbourne   Sydney

Published by the Press Syndicate of the University of Cambridge
The Pitt Building, Trumpington Street, Cambridge CB2 1RP
40 West 20th Street, New York, NY 10011, USA
10 Stamford Road, Oakleigh, Melbourne 3166, Australia

First published 1990

Printed in Great Britain at the University Press, Cambridge

British Library cataloguing in publication data
Gransden, K. W. (Karl Watts), *1925–*
Virgil: the Aeneid. – (Landmarks of world
literature)
1. Epic poetry in Latin. Virgil, Aeneid – Critical
studies
I. Title   II. Series
873′.01

Library of Congress cataloguing in publication data
Virgil, the Aeneid / K. W. Gransden.
    p.   cm. – (Landmarks of world literature)
ISBN 0–521–32329–0. – ISBN 0–521–31157–8 (paperback)
1. Virgil, Aeneid.   2. Aeneas (Legendary character) in
literature.   I. Title.   II. Series.
PA6825.G688   1990
873′.01–dc20   89–22273 CIP

ISBN 0 521 32329 0 hard covers
ISBN 0 521 31157 8 paperback

Contents

Preface

After more than twenty-five years of reading, teaching and writing about the *Aeneid*, I am conscious of a considerable and not easily definable pile-up of debt. It is not easy to distinguish the help and advice I have received in respect of previous and forthcoming publications on Virgil from those specifically sought in relation to the present book; but I am gratefully aware that Professor E. J. Kenney, Dr N. Horsfall and the late R. D. Williams have helped me, in many ways and over many years, to understand Virgil better. I must also thank Dr Peter Stern for his careful scrutiny both of an early draft of this book and of the finished manuscript. As for the secondary literature on the *Aeneid*, which is of course enormous, I have been fortunate to receive, for the purpose of review, many recent books on Virgil, for which I am grateful to the editors of the *Classical Review*, *The Times Higher Educational Supplement* and *The Modern Language Review*.

One might be daunted by all this, were it not that 'the last word' can never be written about a great text concerned with the meaning of history and the life and suffering of humanity, and I have tried in this book, while drawing freely on the researches of my predecessors, to develop some approaches to the poem which I attempted in an earlier publication, *Virgil's Iliad*, and which in some respects differ from the traditional procedures of classical exegesis.

Chapter 1

Background

1 Virgil in the light of his time

Virgil's *Aeneid* has almost certainly generated a longer and larger tradition of commentary than any other poem in the European canon. A critic who offers to add to this enormous accretion might take as his starting point a reflection by Frank Kermode (*Forms of Attention*, 1985): 'since we have no experience of a venerable text that ensures its own perpetuity, we may reasonably say that the medium in which it survives is commentary'. The *Aeneid*, a venerable text if ever there was one, has been subjected to a continual process of revaluation from the fourth century AD until our own time. Consequently, while remaining as it always was, it has undergone successive transformations which have had the effect of making it seem perpetually modern, and which have in a sense become part of the totality of the text as experienced by the reader. Translation, as well as critical commentary, 'appreciation' and interpretation, must be included in this process of transformation and accretion.

The poem's unique place as a landmark in European letters is partly owing to historical circumstances. On 2 September 31 BC Gaius Julius Octavianus, adopted son and heir of the assassinated and deified Julius Caesar, defeated Mark Antony and Cleopatra at the battle of Actium – events familar to English readers from Shakespeare's play – and emerged as *princeps*, nominally first citizen but effectively sole ruler, of the Roman world. It was a decisive moment in history. About a year later, Virgil, then aged forty, began work on the *Aeneid*, and included in the poem's eighth book a splendid panegyric of this victory: his treatment is epic, not history, and shows how in the space of a few years Actium had become, in the words of Sir Ronald Syme (*The Roman Revolution*) 'the birth legend in the mythology of the principate'.

In 27 BC Octavian received the title of Augustus and established peace throughout the Roman world. It was a peace not without local interruptions and campaigns in Europe and the east, but for the Romans it was a true peace, for it marked the end of civil strife in Italy after decades of power-struggles between rival leaders. In unifying Italy Augustus achieved something which in modern times was not to happen again until the nineteenth century.

During the years preceding Actium Virgil had completed his *Georgics*, a poem about agriculture full of praise of the fruitfulness of the Italian countryside: in the words of a modern translator of the poem, C. Day Lewis, he 'sang in time of war the arts of peace'. But the first book of the *Georgics* had ended with a powerful evocation of a nation torn by the horrors of civil war − *saevit toto Mars impius orbe*, 'wicked war rages over the whole earth' − and a prayer to the gods to allow Octavian to come as saviour of his generation:

> hunc saltem everso iuvenem succurrere saeclo
> ne prohibete
> Forbid not this young man from coming to rescue at last
> Our ruined generation

The 'Pax Augusta' was marked by an expensive religious programme of rebuilding and restoration in Rome: temples and altars of victory and thanksgiving were erected, notably the splendid marble temple of Apollo on the Palatine (remains of which can still be seen) built alongside Augustus' own house and dedicated on 9 October 28 BC. Taking poet's licence, Virgil imagined in the eighth book of the *Aeneid* that this temple was already finished in 29 BC when Augustus celebrated a triple triumph, in commemoration of victories in Illyricum, Egypt and Actium itself; he depicts the *princeps* reviewing the parade of conquered peoples on the steps of this temple:

> at Caesar triplici invectus Romana triumpho
> moenia, dis Italis uotum immortale sacrabat,

maxima ter centum totam delubra per urbem . . .
ipse sedens niveo candentis limine Phoebi
dona recognoscit populorum . . .
incedunt victae longo ordina gentes . . .
But Caesar, riding in triple triumph into the city,
Made a solemn and undying vow to the gods of Italy –
Three hundred great temples throughout the city . . .
He himself sitting on the snow-white steps of shining Apollo's
  temple
Acknowledges the gifts of the people . . .
and the defeated nations pass in long procession.

Here too Virgil takes poetic licence, for in his autobiography *Res Gestae* (Things Achieved) Augustus says he built twelve new temples and restored eighty-two others. These acts of *pietas* (observance of what is due towards gods and men) were of the greatest importance. The Romans seem understandably to have felt that the years of civil bloodshed they had experienced were a kind of curse going back to Romulus' legendary killing of his brother Remus and perhaps even further back to an act of impiety by King Laomedon of Troy, who was said to have withheld payment promised to the gods for building the walls of Troy; Virgil refers to this in the *Georgics*:

satis iam pridem sanguine nostro
Laomedonteae luimus periuria Troiae.
We have long ago sufficiently expiated
the perjury of Laomedon's Troy.

(*Georgics* 1. 501–2)

The hero of the *Aeneid*, Aeneas, was himself a Trojan who escaped from the ruins of Troy when the gods themselves helped the Greeks to destroy the walls they had once built: this is described in *Aeneid* II, the tale of the fall of Troy. The Romans sometimes attributed their own misfortunes to want of *pietas*, whence Virgil's emphasis of this quality in his hero, *pius Aeneas*. Virgil's contemporary, the poet Horace, also says that until the temples which have been allowed to fall into neglect and desecration are restored and rededicated, the sins of the fathers will continue to be visited on the children.

Augustus died in AD 14, having by then laid the foundations of the Julio-Claudian dynasty and thus in effect, succeeding where his adoptive father Julius Caesar had failed, established the Roman Empire. During his reign another event occurred, of greater importance to the world than the battle of Actium. By one of history's significant accidents Virgil's celebration of the Pax Augusta coincided with the birth of Christ, the Prince of Peace, 'the still point of the turning world' (in T. S. Eliot's phrase). Thus the Romans' heartfelt belief that at last, in the words of Shakespeare in *Antony and Cleopatra*, 'the time of universal peace is near', was justified in the temporal world a few years before the unique, unrepeatable transition from paganism to Christianity, though it was to be several centuries before the Roman empire officially adopted the new religion. Throughout nearly the whole of its 2,000 years of life the *Aeneid* has been read in a Christian context, and its celebration of the Pax Augusta could be seen as inaugurating a new order of time and history. This reading reached its zenith in the middle ages when Virgil was revered as a 'magus' and as '*anima naturaliter Christiana*', a naturally Christian soul, appearing as Dante's guide through hell and purgatory in his *Divine Comedy* (see below, pp. 105–107); but it has been revived, albeit with different premises, by modern critics, e.g. Frank Kermode in his book *The Classic*.

In *Aeneid* VI the shade of Aeneas' father Anchises reveals to his son, in the Elysian fields, the future heroes of Rome, culminating in Augustus:

> hic vir, hic est, tibi quem promitti saepius audis,
> Augustus Caesar, divi genus, aurea condet
> saecula qui rursus Latio regnata per arva
> Saturno quondam, super et Garamantes et Indos
> proferet imperium; iacet extra sidera tellus,
> extra anni solisque vias, ubi caelifer Atlas
> axem umero torquet stellis ardentibus aptum . . .
> . . . nec vero Alcides tantum telluris obivit.
> This is the man, this is he, so often promised you,
> Augustus Caesar, of race divine, who shall
> Establish again in Latium the golden race
> In the fields where Saturn reigned. He shall extend
> His empire beyond the Africans and the Indians,
> To a land beyond the zodiac and the paths of the solar year
> Where on his shoulders heaven-bearing Atlas
> Revolves the world's axis studded with blazing stars . . .
> Not even Hercules travelled so far.

The 'Messianic' tone and language of this passage are impossible to ignore. In addition, in a short pastoral poem (the fourth eclogue) written long before the *Aeneid*, in 40 BC, Virgil tells of the imminent birth of a boy-child of divine origin who shall rule over a world to which peace and justice shall return, and restore the golden age. Some of the imagery of this poem is found in other prophetic literature (see further below, 14–16).

The idea that Augustus was the 'promised saviour' of his people is firmly rooted in the various 'saviour cults' of the first century BC, of which only Christianity was destined to survive. One such was Hercules, to whom Augustus is compared in the passage quoted above. These saviour-heroes laboured on behalf of civilisation, ridding the world of various manifestations of evil and barbarism – they are sometimes called 'culture-heroes' – and were eventually deified.

One such exploit of Hercules, his slaying of a fire-breathing monster called Cacus, took place, according to a legend which Virgil uses in *Aeneid* VIII, on the very site of the future Rome, on the Aventine hill. Hercules was subsequently deified and was worshipped in Rome at the Great Altar of Hercules which survived into imperial times. Virgil imagines the cult to have already started in the heroic age of Aeneas. His description of the ritual bears some resemblance to the corporate ceremonies of Christian communion: the shared feast, the wine, the hymn, the prayer, the deity who will come to help those in need; the phrase Virgil uses to describe how Hercules came to those in danger, *auxilium adventumque dei*, has an almost liturgical ring, and the same word *adventus* is used also of Augustus in *Aeneid* VI.

The poet Horace also refers to Augustus' divine origin and divine destiny: *serus in caelum redeas*, 'may you return late to heaven', he writes in Odes 1.2; in Odes 3.5 he is more fulsome: *praesens divus habebitur/Augustus adiectis Britannis/imperio gravibusque Persis*. 'With the addition of Britain and Persia to the empire, Augustus will be accepted as god made manifest.' In Odes 3.3 Horace visualised Augustus drinking nectar with Hercules and Bacchus, another 'culture-hero' who according to legend brought the arts of civilisation, including viniculture, to the East. In Epistles 2.1 Horace provides a useful register of these culture-heroes and their achievements.

> Romulus et Liber pater et cum Castore Pollux
> post ingentia facta deorum in templa recepti,
> dum terras hominumque colunt genus, aspera bella
> componunt, agros assignant, oppida condunt,
> ploravere suis non respondere favorem
> speratum meritis . . . exstinctus amabitur idem.
> praesenti tibi maturos largimur honores,
> iurandasque tuum per numen ponimus aras,
> nil oriturum alias, nil ortum tale fatentes.
> Romulus and father Bacchus, Castor and Pollux,
> After mighty deeds were received into the temples of the gods;
> But while they were [performing these deeds], civilising
>   nations and men,
> Ending wars, redistributing land, founding cities,
> They felt it keenly that they received no favours
> Corresponding to their deserts . . . You have to be dead to be
>   loved.
> But to you [Augustus] we pay due honours in good time,
> While you are still among us, to you we set up altars,
> And we admit that none like you will ever come or ever came.

The old culture-heroes had to wait till they were dead to be celebrated: in Pope's words, 'these suns of glory please not till they set'. Augustus did not have to wait. It should be remembered that this poem was written some years after Virgil's death, when the 'personality cult' of Augustus had grown, and that this poem is intended as panegyric or 'praise of Caesar'.

All the great culture-heroes were notable for fighting against barbarism on behalf of civilisation. The fight between Hercules and Cacus in *Aeneid* VIII is a paradigm of many such encounters. They have their literary origin in the mythical battles of Zeus and the Olympian deities (who were always presented by the poets Homer and Hesiod anthropomorphically, possessed of great physical beauty and strength) against various giants, monsters, centaurs, Amazons, at the very dawn of time. All these encounters might be seen as examples of an eternal conflict between order and disorder, good and evil, light and dark. By the time we reach Homer, these encounters have become more humanistic, though there remains Achilles' extraordinary fight with the river-god in *Iliad* XXI, and, in the *Odyssey*, various engagements in which the rational hero outwits a one-eyed giant, a witch, a magic whirlpool, etc. When we reach the *Aeneid*, the description of the battle of Actium in book VIII is presented as a fight between the Olympian deities on the side of Augustus, and the dog-headed monsters of Egyptian worship, on the side of Cleopatra.

Aeneas himself, the hero of Virgil's epic, fits into this sequence of culture-heroes. His principal enemy in the poem, Turnus, is not monstrous or barbarous, though he is depicted as irrational, hotheaded, selfish and self-vaunting. Virgil takes even further Homer's tendency to present both sides of a conflict with dignity and humanity. Nevertheless, Aeneas' civilising mission is emphasised throughout. The role of the saviour was not merely to rid the world of evil, but also to build some positive and lasting good. 'Not by conquest alone, but by the founding of a lasting city, did a hero win divine honours in life and divinity after death' (Syme); Horace, in the passage quoted above, lists the founding of cities as one of the civilizing achievements of the culture-hero. The real theme of the *Aeneid*, as was clear to its earliest readers, was the founding of Rome and its subsequent rise, under Augustus, to its greatest glory. In this respect Aeneas could be seen as a prefiguration of Augustus himself. The labours of Aeneas are presented as the first stage of a mighty endeavour which will later call on the efforts of Romulus and the great heroes of the republic, and which will culminate in the triumph of Augustus: *tantae molis erat Romanam condere gentem*: 'so great a toil it was to found the Roman nation' (*Aeneid*, I.33).

2 Life of Virgil

Publius Vergilius Maro was born on 15 October 70 BC (the traditional date, though according to Dante he was born in

July, see *Inferno* 1.70) at Andes, a village near Mantua, the modern Pietole; he died at Brindisi on 20 September 19 BC. He was buried near Naples, on the road to Pozzuoli: a tomb purporting to be his can still be seen. The spelling of his name in antiquity was Vergilius. But by AD 400 the spelling Virgilius had begun to creep in: perhaps by corruption through the kind of popular and usually false etymology the Romans themselves had been so fond of. The new spelling might suggest a connection both with *virga*, the rod by which the god Hermes 'Guide of Souls' marshalled the souls of the dead to the underworld − a reference to the poet's own role as the magus of *Aeneid* VI in which Aeneas is led to the underworld − and with *virgo*: Virgil was nicknamed Parthenias, 'Maiden', in his own lifetime, rather as Milton was nicknamed 'Our Lady of Christ's' at Cambridge. Virgil never married and may have had homosexual inclinations: although the presence of homosexual themes in the *Eclogues* is a traditional characteristic of the pastoral genre, deriving from Greek exemplars, the intense mutual affection of the young Trojan heroes Nisus and Euryalus in *Aeneid* IX does seem more evidently homo-erotic than, say, the friendship of Achilles and Patroclus in Homer's *Iliad*.

The new spelling ousted the older, correct Latin spelling and passed into the English and French vernaculars as Virgil(e). It is a common though misguided piece of pedantry to spell his name in English as Vergil, though his Latin name is nowadays always correctly spelt Vergilius.

A biography of Virgil was written during the reign of Trajan (AD 117–38) by Suetonius. This survives in a version by Aelius Donatus (4th century AD), whose commentary on Virgil apart from this *Life* and a preface, is lost; but it was used by another critic, Servius, who also wrote in the 4th century AD and whose monumental commentary does survive, both in its original form and in an expanded form first published by the French scholar Pierre Daniel in 1600. The additional matter in this longer version may represent parts of the earlier commentary by Donatus. The Donatus *Life* lists various juvenile writings of the poet, but these are nowadays regarded (with one or two possible rather than probable exceptions) as spurious imitations written shortly after the poet's death: they are included in the ancient manuscripts and are known as the Appendix Vergiliana. It is generally assumed that the canon of the poet's authentic compositions consists of three books: the *Eclogues*, the *Georgics* and the *Aeneid*.

Virgil was by temperament shy and retiring and made no mark on Roman public life. He was brought up in the country and educated at Cremona, Milan, and Rome, where he studied rhetoric, and was preparing for a legal and political career, which he soon abandoned, retiring to Naples when the civil war broke out (49 BC) to study philosophy, his first, and, as tradition tells us concerning his plans for his old age, last love. His father lost his land during the 'dispossessions', when land was redistributed by the triumvirate of Lepidus, Antony and Octavian (as he then still was) to returning veterans after the campaign of Philippi (42 BC). The poet himself may also have been temporarily dispossessed and had his land restored through 'friends in high places', though this episode is speculative and is based on the scenarios of the first and ninth eclogues, which should not be read as literal autobiography.

Virgil was also a friend of Horace and of other poets, notable in their day, whose work does not survive or survives only in fragments, including Cinna, Gallus and Varius; the last-named, together with Plotius Tucca, edited the *Aeneid* for publication after Virgil's death. These writers made up a literary circle which was linked to Augustus through his friend and counsellor Maecenas, a notable patron of the arts and a friend both of Virgil, who dedicated his second work, the *Georgics*, to him, and of Horace, who refers to him frequently: in his fifth satire he describes a journey to Brindisi made in the company of Maecenas, Varius, Tucca and Virgil, 'than whom purer souls never breathed, nor any to whom I am closer'; and in his tenth satire he says that he writes for the discriminating few and that it is enough for him if Plotius, Varius, Maecenas, Virgil and several other chosen spirits like his work.

Virgil began the composition of his greatest work, the *Aeneid*, around 29 BC. A few years later its progress was arousing such expectancy that the poet Propertius wrote:

> nescio quid maius nascitur Iliade
> something greater than the *Iliad* is in the making.

In the year 26 BC Augustus wrote to Virgil from Spain that he had not yet seen the outline of the poem or any passage from it; but a few years later the poet read books II, IV, and VI to Augustus and his circle. In 19 BC Virgil left Italy to travel to Greece, intending to spend a further three years revising and polishing the *Aeneid* and then to devote the rest of his life to the study of philosophy. In the event, he never carried out that plan. He met Augustus in Athens, and was persuaded to return home with him. He fell ill at Megara after going sightseeing on a hot day. He embarked for Italy none the less, and died at Brindisi on 20 Sept. All details in this paragraph are taken from the ancient *Life*, as is the tradition that he first tried to persuade Varius to burn the manuscript of the *Aeneid* if anything should happen to him, but that Varius refused to give any undertaking; in the event Virgil left the manuscript to Varius and Tucca, who published the poem on Augustus' instructions. They evidently did very little editing, since the fifty-odd incomplete lines which it contains (and which support the statement that he intended to revise the whole text) were reproduced as they stood, and do so to this day; though some ancient scholars did make attempts to complete them, these were never accepted into the text. It should however be emphasised that the poem, though unrevised, is in no sense incomplete or unfinished (as Spenser's *Faerie Queene* is unfinished). We know, also from the ancient *Life*, that Virgil first wrote a prose draft of the whole work, then began to compose it passage by passage, not necessarily in the order of the twelve books, so that some portions of the earlier books may well have been written after some of the later sections. But it is to be observed that nothing from the second half of the poem is recorded as having been read to Augustus.

3 The Eclogues

The *Aeneid* draws continually on the past: not only on earlier Greek and Latin epic poetry but also on its author's own previous compositions. A brief account of these earlier works is therefore necessary. The first publication was the collection of ten short pastoral eclogues (only two of them exceed 100 lines in length) called in Latin *Bucolica*, and modelled on the *Idylls* of Theocritus, the Greek poet of the third century BC, who is the earliest known exponent of the genre. Virgil's eclogues were probably originally issued separately or in pairs (Coleman 15), though the precise order and date of their composition remains speculative: none is likely to be earlier than 42 BC or later than 37 BC. Each poem is a self-contained artefact, but it seems probable that Virgil planned a set of poems from the start. Six of the poems, nos. 2, 3, 4, 5, 7 and 8 are either dedicated to, or in some way connected with, the historian Asinius Pollio, who according to the ancient Life first proposed to Virgil that he should try his hand at pastoral; these form the core of the book. The other four eclogues seem from internal evidence to have been added later to make up the set of ten. The first is evidently a 'programme' poem written as an introduction to the whole work; both it and the ninth eclogue contain references to the land confiscations which may have affected the poet personally (see above, p. 9). The ninth eclogue also contains echoes and reminiscences of other poems in the set. The tenth eclogue was clearly written as an end piece to the whole book; it is the poet's farewell to pastoral, and also contains echoes of no. 1. The sixth eclogue is the most difficult and least pastoral of the ten, a proclamation of new literary allegiances, to Hesiod and Callimachus rather than Theocritus; here Virgil is already experimenting with other genres. It is dedicated to Alfenus Varus, who served with Pollio as a land commissioner, and contains references to the elegiac poet Cornelius Gallus, whose unrequited love-affair forms the sad theme of the final eclogue.

These beguiling, deceptively simple yet elusively complex

little poems have had an influence out of all proportion to their modest size. That size, that small compass, was itself something of a literary manifesto: the *deductum carmen*, the 'thin spun', slight poem, was the ideal not only of Theocritus but of another Alexandrian poet, Callimachus, to whom Virgil alludes in the sixth eclogue, which begins with a *recusatio*, a literary apologia, a refusal to tackle large heroic themes such as military campaigns:

> agrestem tenui meditabor harundine Musam
> I shall exercise my rustic muse on a slender reed.

This line is itself echoed in the first line of eclogue 1:

> Tityre, tu patulae recubans sub tegmine fagi
> silvestrem tenui musam meditaris avena.
> Tityrus, you lying at your ease under the spreading beech
> Exercise your pastoral muse on a slender reed.

Tenuis, 'slight', was a key word of Alexandrian literary precept and practice, and marked a reaction against the cumbersome epics written in imitation of Homer.

Pastoral was a self-consciously sophisticated genre, autonomous and self-reflexive, in which characters purporting to be shepherds were often poets in thin allegorical disguise. It was the product of metropolitan cultures with nostalgic hankerings for rural simplicity, and for an idealised 'Arcadian' landscape where one could pass the time singing songs, making and celebrating love or lamenting it when unrequited, and discussing poetry. The ideal landscape was that of mediterranean urban man: cool shade, the sound of water – the rhetorical topos which became classified as the 'locus amoenus' (pleasant place) where one could forget the world of labour and pursue leisure (*otium*, the Latin word, is the opposite of *negotium*, business) and personal relationships. When occasionally in the *Eclogues* (e.g. no. 2) a character wanders out of this ideal place into the wild woods and the deserted mountain side, this is a conscious reflection of his own emotional dislocation. It is this correspondence between personal emotion and external landscape which first clearly enters European poetry with Virgil's eclogues and which has made them of such significance to their successors.

But it is not only the despair of unrequited love which invades the placid world of Arcadian *otium* presented in the *Eclogues*. Virgil related this world to the harsh realities of contemporary politics; in particular to the policy of land confiscations which had been operating intermittently ever since Philippi and continued after Actium. Eclogues 1 and 9, which treat of these dispossessions, seem to include disguised figures of the poet himself, and have since ancient times intrigued critics. We must, however, be careful not to take such 'autobiographical' elements too literally. What is important to us is that the theme of exile seemed to move the poet deeply and that he treated it with profound insight and subtlety, entering into the sadness of the dispossessed:

> nos patriae finis et dulcia linquimus arva,
> nos patriam fugimus.
> we leave the pleasant fields and farms,
> we leave our home.

I have deliberately used, in that translation, the echo of Virgil's words in Tennyson's *In Memoriam* CII:

> We leave the well beloved place . . . My feet are set
> To leave the pleasant fields and farms.

Virgil also records the heartfelt relief of those whose farms are saved by official decree. In particular, the first eclogue celebrates the *libertas* of the pastoral poet (his freedom to write as he pleases, to indulge in art for art's sake) in terms of political freedom, salvation from exile conferred by Octavian, hailed in the poem as *deus*. Only one with divine attributes, says 'Tityrus', could offer such largesse; his friend Meliboeus, however, has been less successful; no intervention from on high has saved him, he must go into exile. Like many of the eclogues, the first is a dramatic dialogue (between the lucky Tityrus and the unlucky Meliboeus). The ninth eclogue is on the same theme, but is much sadder: for here Virgil articulates the artist's awareness that sometimes art itself, as well as farming, can be a 'casualty of war' (Coleman, 273).

Attempts to recall fragments of pastoral song avail nothing in this poem, and the fragments serve only to intensify the sense of loss and waste: *nunc oblita mihi tot carmina*, 'now I have forgotten so many songs,' are among the most moving words in the entire collection.

The fourth eclogue deserves special mention for quite a different reason (it has been briefly alluded to above, p. 5). It is a political and philosophical prophecy; there are no characters, no dialogue, but the poet speaks in his own voice, addressing Pollio in the year of his consulship (40 BC). The poem extends the usual modest parameters of the pastoral genre: *paulo maiora canamus*, says the poet, let us sing a somewhat grander song: that 'somewhat' is self-consciously imitated by Milton when he, too, sets out in *Lycidas* to extend the range of pastoral elegy: 'begin, and somewhat loudly sweep the strings'.

The fourth eclogue describes the imminent birth of a boy, a divine child who shall move among both gods and mortals, and in whose lifetime the golden age associated with Saturn, who ruled the universe before Jupiter, will return. St Augustine suggested that the boy referred to Christ and that Virgil had come across the prophecy in the Sibylline oracles. Certainly the apocalyptic imagery of the poem has an oracular tone. It also possesses a high proportion of end-stopped lines, and other stylistic features, such as repetition, rhyme and formulaic phrasing, which can be paralleled in Sybylline oracular texts. The Sibyl of Cumae prophesies to Aeneas in *Aeneid* VI (see below) and prophecies associated with her were written down and consulted periodically, as part of the Roman state religion. Some of these texts survive, but they are of a much later date than Virgil and are of doubtful authenticity. They may have been influenced by Jewish prophetic writing. This would account for similarities between Virgil's fourth eclogue and Isaiah: 'the cattle shall not fear the lion' occurs in the eclogue, in Isaiah 11.6, and in the Sibylline oracles. The last two also employ the phrase 'and a little child shall lead them', and although this is not in Virgil, the sense that the child will be a ruler is strong in the poem: *pacatumque reget . . . orbem*, 'he shall rule a world at peace'.

What is striking about this poem is not whether we should accept that Virgil had read pre-Christian prophetic texts (it is improbable that he could have read the Hebrew of Isaiah), but the poem's vision of a universal regeneration and the proposition that the golden age, traditionally located in a lost and irrecoverable order of time past, will return. The Greek poet Hesiod, in his poem *Works and Days*, articulated the myth of the five races of man, a declining and irreversible sequence from gold to iron, ending with a gloomy forecast that the present iron race will degenerate still further when grey-haired babies are born 'and there will be no help against evil'. Virgil reverses this: *his* baby will grow up to preside over a world in which the last traces of evil will linger for a while and then disappear. In the context of the saviour figure of Augustus, the nostalgic optimism of the fourth eclogue can be related to certain passages in the *Aeneid*, especially Jupiter's prophecy in book I, which uses the same apocalyptic imagery to foretell an age of universal peace:

> aspera tum positis mitescent saecula bella
> The fierce generations will grow gentle, wars being ended.

The word *saecula* also occurs in the fourth eclogue, and belongs to the Roman sybilline tradition. A *saeculum* was a period of time, 100 or 110 years. The *ludi saeculares* were fixed after consultation of the Sibylline books; these games were celebrated by Augustus in 19 BC and Horace wrote his *Carmen saeculare* for the occasion. Horace's poem takes the form of a hymn to Apollo, presiding deity of Troy, Augustus and Rome; in Virgil's poem the 'reign of Apollo' will precede the return of the age of Saturn, the golden age proper.

It must be emphasised that there is no evidence, and little likelihood, that Virgil was referring in this poem to Christ. Nor indeed, since it was written in 40 BC, could the reference be to Augustus himself, then still a minor partner of Mark Antony, although in the *Aeneid* his coming is 'prophesied' by Anchises in similar Messianic language (see above, p. 4). Other candidates have been proposed, including Marcellus, briefly Augustus' adopted heir (he died in 23 BC).

The identity of the child was a subject of speculation even in Virgil's lifetime, and it is unlikely that the mystery will ever be solved. What we do know is that the two *topoi* it develops, the 'Wonder-Child' and the golden age, were both accessible to Virgil in his time; the latter, indeed, was evidently of special interest to Pollio; it also figures in *Eclogues* 3 and 8 (both addressed to Pollio). Another *topos*, that of the good ruler, goes back to Homer (*Odyssey*, 19. 108–14) and Hesiod; while the prophecy of a glorious offspring is traditionally part of the epithalamium or marriage-hymn, cf. Catullus 64, to which Virgil was certainly indebted. But the eclogue remains unique and *sui generis*, summing up, in powerful metaphors still relevant to us today, the recurrent hopes and dreams of mankind.

4 The Georgics

Virgil's second composition, the *Georgics*, was again inspired by a Greek model, the didactic 'wisdom' poetry of the Boeotian poet Hesiod, who probably lived a generation or so after Homer. The *Georgics* is a poem about agriculture (the Greek title is from *georgos*, a farmer), including the care of livestock, bees and vines, but again Virgil has pushed the limits of the genre further than his predecessors, who also include Varro, the Roman writer on agriculture. If the theme of the *Eclogues* was *otium*, the leisure and freedom to write as one pleased – a freedom which could only operate under certain political guarantees – the theme of the *Georgics* is *labor improbus*, which might be translated 'damned hard work'. The poem is in four books, totalling 2,188 verses. In book 1, Virgil describes how Jupiter took away from man the benefits of the first golden age – fruits available for the plucking, honey on tap, 'all men idle, all', as Shakespeare's Gonzalo puts it in his picture of the golden age in *The Tempest*, and made man work for his bread by the sweat of his brow, as after the Fall in Genesis, when Adam and Eve were expelled from their *locus amoenus*, the earthly paradise. In the new dispensation of Jupiter, nature still collaborated with man, especially in naturally blessed and fruitful Italy, but man was now an equal partner: without his efforts the land would revert to the wild, weeds would choke the crops, the vines be blighted, the cattle die.

This motif of hard work offers no nostalgic vision of a return to the golden age, as in the fourth eclogue; but in his portrait in the second *Georgic* of the self-sufficient Italian farmer, at peace on his own land, living the good life, Virgil saw another and different metaphor for the ideal society. He thus showed up an ambiguity in the whole *topos* of the golden age, which has haunted poets and visionaries through the ages. The golden age offers man a vision of happiness without the need for toil; yet, once that age has ended, if work continues to be seen as a curse, nothing will ever be achieved in the real world. Virgil sees the life of the Italian farmer as itself a version of the legendary 'good old days' when Saturn, exiled from Olympus by his usurping son Jupiter, was said to have taken refuge in Italy and there recreated the golden age over which he had once presided: *aureus hanc vitam in terris Saturnus agebat*, 'this was the life that golden Saturn led in our land'. Virgil picks up this theme in *Aeneid* VIII, in which the Arcadian settler Evander, now living on the site of what was one day to be Rome, explains to Aeneas how Saturn came to Italy and established peace there:

> aurea quae perhibent illo sub rege fuere
> saecula: sic placida populos in pace regebat.
> The centuries they call golden were under that king:
> He ruled the people in unbroken peace.

Thus the life of the farmer in Italy was a symbiosis of natural fruitfulness and human energy and resourcefulness. A recurring motif of the golden age *topos* (it is found in Eclogue 4) is that men did not construct ships to cross the sea, import costly delicacies or mine for gold, for the golden age was golden in a metaphorical not a literal sense (a metaphor which goes back to Plato): Virgil's farmer does none of these things; he operates a kind of self-sufficient village economy which has been a dream of man ever since, especially as technologies have become more complex. Moreover, the Stoic philosophy of being content with a modest livelihood was used by Virgil in *Georgics* 2 to criticize the growing wealth of the metropolitan Rome of his own day, which imported many costly and superfluous luxuries. Virgil saw a correlation between material excess and moral decline; his praises of rural Italy in the *Georgics* show the farmer's life as morally sounder than the city-dweller's.

The *Georgics*, with its emphasis on hard work and traditional virtues, may be seen as a transitional poem leading us to the *Aeneid* and the epic labours of the great saviour-hero Aeneas. Its real subject is not so much the practical details and advice on agriculture, though Virgil does include these, and the idea of a verse-handbook sounds sillier to us than it would have done in the first century BC; ancient handbooks were written in verse (albeit not as sophisticated as Virgil's) long before they were written in prose. The poet's true subject is the praise of Italy, of its farmers and of the exploitation of the natural resources of the land. These resources had been available in the first golden age, but without any incentive to improve them; what is already created perfect by divine act cannot be improved, which is why Hesiod, in his myth of the five successive races of man, presents a decline from pristine perfection, whereas Virgil often prefers to follow his predecessor Lucretius in seeing man's progress, as we do today, in evolutionary terms, a move from primitivism to civilisation. But Virgil, like Augustus himself, thought the progress of civilisation had gone too far towards excess.

The *Georgics*, it should be remembered, was written in a time of war. Man's struggle to improve his environment is never ending, and war disrupts this process, turning ploughshares into swords. The virtues of the Italian farmer appear again in the *Aeneid* in the 'Spartan' virtues of the aboriginal Italians whom the Trojans under Aeneas encountered when they landed in Italy.

I have called the *Georgics* a transitional poem, and this is true of its technique and style as well as of its subject matter. The didactic mode is enriched and enlivened by various devices which we associate with heroic epic verse, such as similes and narrative digressions: for instance, the famous story of Orpheus and Eurydice, familiar to us from the operatic stage, is movingly told to form the climax of the whole work. In this tale of how a legendary 'culture hero', a poet and singer, descended into the underworld on a sad vain quest, for there are limits to what even great heroes can achieve, Virgil not only returned to the theme of art's limitations, touched on in *Eclogue* 9, but also looked forward to the *Aeneid*. The story of Orpheus in *Georgics* 4 contains verses which Virgil was to use again in *Aeneid* VI, Aeneas' descent into the underworld.

The battle of the bees in *Georgics* 4 is also notable for its epic treatment:

> nam saepe duobus
> regibus incessit magno discordia motu.
> . . . for often civil strife arises
> Between two kings amidst a mighty upheaval.

This passage has been seen as an allusion to the rivalry between Augustus and Antony. It seems clear that the notion that he would one day have to write an epic was already knocking, so to say, on the door of Virgil's creative mind. In a passage at the beginning of *Georgics* 3 he expressly refers to Augustus and to a projected literary monument to his achievements.

> In medio mihi Caesar erit, templumque tenebit
> In the middle [of my song] I shall have Caesar, he shall have the temple.

This is the 'temple of song', a metaphor first used by the Greek poet Pindar, and Virgil seems to have had in mind some sort of panegyric of Augustus' victories; indeed, such a panegyric did eventually find its way into the *Aeneid*, in the extremely grand and hyperbolic presentation of the battle of Actium 'prophetically' engraved by the god Vulcan on Aeneas' shield. But meanwhile, Virgil returned to the matter in hand, and to Maecenas, to whom the *Georgics* are dedicated:

> Meanwhile, Maecenas, I shall return to the beasts of the field, and carry out your own not inconsiderable commission. Later

> I shall set myself the task of singing Caesar's wars and
> carry his name far and wide beyond his own time.

It appears that this projected epic on Caesar Augustus' wars,
which might have been composed in the annalistic tradition
of Ennius, the principal Roman epic poet of the republican
era (see below, p. 24), was at some stage abandoned in
favour of the more ambitious work which became the *Aeneid*.
This is not primarily about Augustus at all, but about Aeneas,
but through various technical devices the poet was able to
prefigure the achievements of the *princeps* in a more complex
discourse, in which events separated by a thousand years of
legend and history could be treated synchronically rather than
diachronically.

Just as the last eclogue included a self-quotation from the
first, so in the epilogue to the *Georgics*, an eight-line 'coda',
Virgil 'signs off' as a writer of both didactic and pastoral
verse:

> These things I sang of, field cultivation and livestock,
> and trees, while great Caesar was shaking the Euphrates
> and victorious was settling disputes among the welcoming
> nations on his way to the stars.
> As for me, Virgil, Naples, city of virgins,
> Sweetly in my salad days of unheroic leisure
> Took care of me, and I played my youthful shepherd songs,
> And sang you, Tityrus, under the spreading beech.

That last line echoes the first line of *Eclogue* 1. What other
poet has so self-consciously planned and unified his life's
work? His three compositions, 'of man, of nature, and
of human life' (to borrow a phrase from Wordsworth) form a
structured hierarchical progression, from modest pastoral to
high epic, with didactic epic occupying the middle ground.
The eclogues are art for art's sake, self-referential worlds
depicting a kind of community or college of young poets at
play, in love with love and art, sharing their experiments and
experiences, creating a private world. The *Georgics* are collective and social, man at work replacing man at play; they are
deeply moral where the *Eclogues* were amoral, and clearly
project the old Roman values, Republican in the best sense,

which Augustus wanted to promote and revive. Finally, like Milton 'long choosing and beginning late', Virgil turned from the patriotism of the *Georgics*, with its love of the country-side, to the *Aeneid*, in which that patriotism is set in a larger historical context, showing how the land was first won for civilisation, not by the plough but by the sword, a labour which in the poet's own day human ambition and violence had caused to be done all over again.

5 Metrical unity and continuity

Perhaps the most obvious way in which Virgil's three compositions, the *Eclogues*, the *Georgics* and the *Aeneid*, are linked is that they are all written in the same metre. The earliest Greek poets, Homer and Hesiod, used the dactylic hexameter for their narrative and diactic epics. Other Greek metres followed, lyric, iambic and choric, but it happened that Theocritus, Virgil's chief model for his *Eclogues*, chose the hexameter for his pastoral *Idylls* (he might have picked the more 'conversational' iambic). Thus all three of Virgil's models, Theocritus, Hesiod and Homer, were hexameter poets. This metre established itself in Latin as the appropriate one for epic (it was first used by Ennius, see below) as well as for other kinds of verse, such as satire and epistolary verse (the metre of Horace's Epistle to Augustus, quoted above, p. 6, is hexametrical) and it was a natural choice for the young Virgil when he sought to emulate Theocritean pastoral. The Greek hexameter is largely dactylic, the Latin one uses far more spondees, because of the nature of the Latin language, which has far more long syllables. A dactyl is a foot con-sisting of a long syllable followed by two short ones, a spondee consists of two long syllables. The hexameter con-sists of six 'feet' (six 'beats' to the line) disposed as follows:

$$-vv \ / \ -vv \ / \ -vv \ / \ -vv \ / \ -vv \ / \ - -$$
$$- - / \ - - \ / \ - - \ / \ - - \ / \ -vv \ / \ -v$$

The fact that Virgil's three compositions are all in the same metre naturally facilitates self-quotation, and gives the reader a sense of continuity from work to work. It is possible to trace the development and maturing of Virgil as an artist through his handling of the hexameter. In an analogous way we may trace the development of Shakespeare from his early plays to his late ones through his treatment of the so-called iambic pentameter, a decasyllabic line which corresponds in its centrality and continuity in English prosody to the classical hexameter. (It is interesting to note that this metre, in its unrhymed form, the so-called blank verse line, was first introduced into English verse from Italy during the reign of Henry VIII by the Earl of Surrey for his translation of part of the *Aeneid*.) Like Shakespeare, Virgil moved towards an ever increasing freedom and flexibility in his handling of metre.

The Latin hexameter, like the Greek one, is 'quantitative', as indeed is nearly all ancient poetry: that is, the length of each syllable is fixed and predetermined. Medieval Latin poetry and modern vernacular poetry use a stress-based prosody. Thus, in the line:

> Now is the winter of our discontent

the second syllable of discontent is unstressed, but in Latin verse that syllable would be 'long' because the vowel is followed by two consonants. But Latin was spoken with stresses like any modern language, and the prosody of the hexameter, in consequence, consists of a fixed syllabic pattern of dactyls and spondees which might accord with the actual pronunciation of the words, or might conflict with it. In Virgil's poetry more than in any other Latin poetry, the variety of effects made possible by exploiting coincidence and conflict between quantity and stress is seen at its richest and subtlest.

It happens that there survives an apocryphal opening of the *Aeneid* which is overtly autobiographical. It consists of four lines, stated in the ancient *Life* of Donatus, and Servius' commentary, to have been written by the poet himself but deleted by his editors. They are almost certainly spurious: but whoever wrote them was alert to the habit of self-reference which marks the close of the *Georgics*, and to a sense that Virgil's three poems exhibit a remarkable continuity.

The lines are:

> Ille ego, qui quondam gracili modulatus avena
> carmen, et egressus silvis vicina coegi
> ut quamvis avido parerent arva colono,
> gratum opus agricolis, at nunc horrentia Martis
> arma virumque cano . . .
> I the man who once versified on my slender pastoral pipe
> And then, abandoning the woods, taught my native fields
> To obey the farmer's eager demands, and the poem
> Pleased them, now bristling Arms and the man I sing . . .

The tradition that these lines were Virgil's still flourished in the Renaissance; they are closely imitated by Spenser at the beginning of his epic *The Faerie Queene*:

> Lo I the man, whose Muse whilom did mask,
> As time her taught, in lowly shepherd's weeds,
> Am now enforced a far unfitter task,
> For trumpets stern to change mine oaten reeds
> And sing of knights and ladies' gentle deeds.

The canonical opening of the *Aeneid* was, however, famous enough to have been almost a cliché in antiquity: *arma uirumque*, 'arms and the man', has been found scribbled on the walls of Pompeii, and was quoted as the catchphrase of the epic by Ovid, Persius, Seneca, Martial and Quintilian; it was used as the title of a play by Bernard Shaw.

Chapter 2

Virgil and Homer

6 'Arms and the man'

Other Latin poets before Virgil had written important large-scale hexameter compositions. Lucretius' great didactic epic *De Rerum Natura* ('on the nature of things') was an exposition of the physical universe according to the doctrine of Epicurus: although Virgil reacted against its materialism, he was much indebted to Lucretius' style and technique. Earlier, Quintus Ennius (239–169 BC) had written heroic narrative epic, proudly claiming to be a reincarnation of Homer. His *Annales*, as their name implies, was a chronological record of the story of Rome from the fall of Troy (Virgil's starting-point too, though *his* treatment is not chronological) to the death of Romulus. There were eighteen books, unfinished at their author's death, of which only fragments survive, but enough to show that Virgil often echoes the grand cadences and phrases of his predecessor.

But in composing the *Aeneid* Virgil deliberately departed from the annalistic tradition. His masterstroke was to see in the story of Aeneas an opportunity to create a structural and thematic reworking of both the epics of Homer. The *Iliad* is a story set in the war between Greeks and Trojans; the *Odyssey* is the story of one Greek hero's homecoming after the sack of Troy. Virgil reversed this sequence: the first half of his epic tells of the journey of the Trojan hero Aeneas after the fall of Troy in search of a homeland, the second half tells of Aeneas' arrival in Italy, of the war he was obliged to fight to establish his settlement, and of his victory over a local chieftain, Turnus. The ancient *Life* of Virgil described the *Aeneid* as *quasi amborum Homeri carminum instar*: 'a sort of counterpart of both the Homeric poems'. The opening words of the *Aeneid* signal this: 'arms and the man', referring both to a theme of warfare and to a poem about the exploits of a single hero — Homer had begun the *Odyssey* 'Tell me of the man, O muse . . .'

In taking Homer as the model for the last and grandest of his three compositions, Virgil rose to the supreme challenge of ancient literature. Homer's supremacy was taken for granted by Greeks and Romans alike, but his immense epics had spawned many imitations which do not survive but which were widely regarded in antiquity as inferior compositions. Their proliferation, however, had led to a reaction against such long works in the Hellenistic or 'Alexandrian' period, when poets such as Callimachus and Theocritus had advocated and practised composition on a much smaller scale. Roman taste from the late republican period was largely 'Alexandrian', showing preferences for a more personal and subjective style, with great emphasis on form and 'finish'. Virgil was by no means immune from Alexandrian influences: his sensibility is, in comparison to Homer's, what we might call romantic, and the elegance, symmetry and musicality of his verse reflects the Alexandrian emphasis on these qualities. Nevertheless, in selecting Homer as his model, he in effect offered an unfashionable manifesto against Alexandrian miniaturism by going back, not to Homer's tedious imitators, the poets of the now lost 'cyclic epics', but to Homer himself, the origin and cornerstone of all ancient poetry and the undisputed master whom no other poet, until Virgil came along, had been able successfully to emulate. For the lost Greek imitators of Homer appear to have simply told their stories, at great length, and with little psychological subtlety; Homer alone, antiquity agreed, offered true insight into humanity and, in his two epics, did more than just chronicle: he offered technically interesting structures and themes, and set a standard which his successors could not match.

7 The Aeneas Legend

In some remarkable lines in *Iliad* 20 Homer tells of a prophecy by the god Poseidon (Neptune in the Roman pantheon) that the Trojan hero Aineias (this is the Greek spelling) 'is destined to survive, that the generation of Dardanus shall not perish . . . and the might of Aineias shall reign over the Trojans, and his sons' sons, who shall be born of their seed hereafter.' This prophecy makes Aeneas unique among the Trojan heroes: not only will he survive the fall of Troy but he will have a special and important future. An entire tradition developed about him: guided by his mother, the goddess Venus — for like Achilles he was semi-divine — he escaped from Troy with his father Anchises, his son Ascanius and his ancestral gods — this was the beginning of the legend of his *pietas* — and after much wandering about the Mediterranean world reached Hesperia (Italy, land of the west) where he settled in Latium, the modern Lazio, the region north of Rome. This story was recorded by the Greek historian Hellanicus (5th century BC) and developed by later writers, both Greek and Roman. Aeneas was chronologically too early to replace Romulus as the founder of Rome, for this traditionally occurred in 751 BC while the fall of Troy is usually placed around 1184 BC. The mythographers accordingly made Aeneas founder of Lavinium and his son Ascanius ruler of Alba Longa, forerunner of Rome, where his descendants continued to rule for 300 years until the birth of Romulus. These details are given in the *Aeneid* by Jupiter in his prophecy of the future of Rome in book I. Virgil says in that passage that Aeneas himself would only rule for three years; his death is not mentioned there, but in book XII Jupiter reminds Juno that Aeneas is destined, like other culture-heroes before him and like Julius and Augustus Caesar after him, for deification:

> Indigetem Aenean scis ipsa et scire fateris
> deberi caelo fatisque ad sidera tolli.
> You know, and you concede the fact, that Aeneas is
> promised to heaven and destined for the stars, to
> become 'Indiges'. (794–5)

Juno, Homer's Hera, was the implacable foe of the Trojans, but even she cannot gainsay Aeneas' manifest destiny. The title under which he would be worshipped, 'Indiges', was reserved for great national heroes who were deified: it is applied by Virgil to Romulus at *Georgics*, 1. 498, and is also used of Aeneas by Livy (1.2.6) who describes his apotheosis at the river Numicius.

Aeneas thus took his place in the Roman pantheon among the local heroes of Rome. The legend enabled Virgil to link his epic with the *Iliad* and, in common with earlier Roman writers (Ennius, Naevius, Fabius Pictor), push back the dawn of civilisation in Latium to the bronze age, thereby balancing the warlike legends of Romulus, son of Mars, with the story of a hero renowned for *pietas*, wanting peace rather than war, a son of Venus.

The fall of Troy is perhaps the most famous event in the ancient world. The surviving Trojans dispersed and settled in various parts of the Graeco–Roman world, a 'diaspora' not wholly dissimilar to that of the Jews. The Aeneas legend was one of many such colonisation stories; there was also a tradition that Odysseus himself came to Italy, and, by a process of assimilation common in such legends, stories about one hero were sometimes attached to another. But Aeneas' combination of military prowess and *pietas*, together with Homer's strangely prophetic lines about him, made him a special case. Rome became in due time the new Troy, risen like the phoenix from the ashes of the destroyed city of Priam; indeed in the perspective of history the fall of Troy could be seen as the necessary precursor of the rise of Rome, and the whole mighty sequence as part of a divine plan, the working out of fate. At the moment we first meet Aeneas, storm-tossed and praying for death, we are reassured, in Jupiter's words of comfort to Venus, the hero's mother, that all shall be well. The *Aeneid* is the story of how 'out of this nettle, danger, we pluck this flower, safety', even though the happy ending, the triumph of Augustus, lay a thousand years beyond the life and labours of the poem's legendary hero.

8 The 'Odyssean' Aeneid

It is clear that Virgil intended his poem to fall into two

'halves', corresponding structurally to the *Odyssey*, which also falls into two halves: *Odyssey* 1 to 12 describes Odysseus' *nostos* or homecoming from Troy; books 13 to 24 describe his actions after arriving home in Ithaca, including the killing of the suitors of his wife Penelope (see Otis 217). The first half of the *Aeneid* (books I to VI) describe Aeneas' journey from Troy to his new home in Italy, while books VII to XII describe his actions in Italy, including his killing of Turnus, a rival suitor to the Italian princess Lavinia who is destined to marry the stranger from across the sea. Thus in one sense the *whole* of the Aeneid might be called 'Odyssean' in that it reflects both the theme and the structure of the Odyssey: it begins *in medias res* (in the middle of the story) as had the Odyssey, and includes a 'flashback' in which the hero narrates his previous adventures to a royal host who has sheltered and succoured him. But there is a further complication, in that the second half of Virgil's poem is about war, its *mise-en-scène* is a battlefield: Odysseus' killing of the suitors at the end of the *Odyssey* is in comparison merely a violent domestic episode which takes place inside Odysseus' own palace. So Virgil turned from the *Odyssey* to the *Iliad* and modelled his last six books on Homer's tragic poem of war. Nor can we oversimplify Virgil's structure by assuming that there is nothing 'Iliadic' in the first six books of the *Aeneid* and nothing 'Odyssean' in the last six. For example, the funeral games celebrated by Achilles in honour of his dead comrade Patroclus in *Iliad* XXIII are transposed by Virgil to *Aeneid* V, and are held to honour the hero's father, Anchises, who died on the journey westward, in Sicily.

In Homer's *Odyssey*, the hero does not appear until book 5, the first four books of the poem being concerned with Odysseus' son Telemachus (these books are sometimes referred to separately as the 'Telemachy'). In book 5 Odysseus is caught in a storm, and fears that his death is near; in soliloquy he wishes he had died with so many of his peers, at Troy:

> O thrice and four times blessed those Danaans who died
> In Troy.

In *Aeneid* I Aeneas is likewise caught in a storm, and he too,

echoing the words of Homer's Odysseus, wishes he had died
at Troy:

> O thrice and four times blessed
> Those whom it befell to die at Troy.

Indeed, the whole of Aeneid I offers remarkable and clearly
intentional parallels with Odyssey 5–8 (it is characteristic of
the two poets that Homer is expansive while Virgil compresses
and tightens the narrative structure). In both poems the hero
appears at the mercy of an angry deity, is shipwrecked and
cast ashore on a friendly coast, is hospitably received and
entertained at a feast, is asked to tell the story of his adventures, and does so in the books which follow (*Odyssey* 9–12,
Aeneid, II–III) in the form of a 'flashback'.

Thematic and structural parallels with, and verbal
references to, Homer, are frequent throughout the *Aeneid*.
They have been collected by G. N. Knauer (*Die Aeneis und
Homer*). Virgil wrote for a readership educated in Greek
literature in a way the modern reader of Virgil is probably
not, but a detailed acquaintance with Homer is not essential
to an appreciation of Virgil, for two reasons: first, the
multitude of specific allusions to Homer do not need to be
identified, provided we remain generally alert to what we may
call Virgil's Homerizing technique; and secondly, despite
Virgil's immense and continuously proclaimed debt to Homer,
the true value of the *Aeneid* lies in its transformations of
Homer, in the way in which the larger themes and values of the
Homeric world are modified by the 'later' sensibility of the
Roman poet. Virgil, after all, saw Homer not as an immediate
but as a remote ancestor, separated from him by nearly eight
centuries of Greek literature which included Plato, the great
Athenian tragic dramatists, and the Alexandrian poets
Callimachus and Apollonius: the latter's short epic, the
Argonautica, gave Virgil some further material which he used
in his 'Odyssean' Aeneid. Two parallels with modern texts may
also be adduced here. Joyce's *Ulysses* is based structurally and
thematically on the *Odyssey*, and originally carried chapter-
headings referring to episodes in Homer. Joyce removed these

later, and the novel can be read without direct knowledge of the *Odyssey;* its difficulties for the modern reader are of a quite different kind, which a detailed knowledge of Homer's text will be unlikely to solve. Or, to take another case, Tennyson's *Idylls of the King* owes much to Malory, but Tennyson's medievalism has been mediated through the poetry of the Romantics and it is probably sufficient for the reader to be generally aware of the poet's source.

Thus in considering the first six books of the *Aeneid* the reader need only keep in mind the predominant theme of the journey from Troy. Odysseus was trying to get home to Ithaca: Homer's epic was a '*nostos*' or homecoming (see Griffin 44–5). Virgil preserves this motif, by using (or perhaps inventing) a tradition that Dardanus, founder of the Trojan royal house, had been born in Italy and had emigrated to Asia Minor, so that Aeneas' arrival in Italy in *Aeneid* VI could be seen as a homecoming, not as an invasion: he came, not as a usurper but as a man claiming his rightful heritage, for he was that *dux externus* (foreign chief) who was destined to rule in Italy.

Virgil also assimilated to Aeneas various adventures of Odysseus recounted by Homer, the Cyclops for instance, and Scylla and Charybdis. Homer's Odysseus, a hero to the Greeks, was a villain to the Trojans, for it was he who devised the stratagem of the wooden horse by which Troy fell. The Trojans actually took the horse inside their walls, breaking them down to get the monstrous object in, believing it to be a sacred talisman, so great was their *pietas*. Thus Odysseus' trick achieved what ten years of siege and the heroic efforts of Achilles and Diomedes failed to achieve, a point made by Aeneas when he recounts the story of Troy's fall in *Aeneid* II.

This flashback, in which the hero narrates his own earlier adventures, is itself modelled on the long narration of Odysseus in *Odyssey* 9–12. After surviving the storm in book I, Aeneas is shipwrecked on the coast of the modern Tunisia, at Carthage, which was to become the city of Hannibal, whom the Romans defeated a hundred and fifty years before the time of Virgil, and, much later, of St Augustine. There he is treated hospitably by the queen, Dido, a widow, and, like himself, an exile and founder of a great city. It is to Dido that Aeneas tells how Troy fell, and while he tells the tale Dido falls in love with him.

The first half of the *Aeneid* reaches three great emotional climaxes in the three even-numbered books II, IV and VI. In book II Aeneas narrates to Dido the events of the last night of Troy. He continues the first person narrative of his journey in book III, while in book IV Virgil resumes authorial narration and describes the fatal passion of Dido for Aeneas and her subsequent suicide. In book V the Trojans continue their journey to Italy, where they arrive at Cumae, near the modern Pozzuoli, on the gulf of Naples. In book VI Aeneas visits the Sibyl of Cumae, a prophetess, who leads him to the underworld. Here he meets the shade of his father, who reveals to him the future greatness of Rome. Odysseus had also visited the world of the dead, in *Odyssey* 11, and had learned something of his own future from the prophet Teiresias. What Anchises reveals to Aeneas is not his own immediate future, but the heroes and events, remote from him in time future, from Romulus to Augustus: the story of the foundation and preservation of Rome. A comparison between *Aeneid* VI and *Odyssey* 11 (see section 15, below) will illustrate how Virgil transformed Homeric themes and motifs.

9 The 'Iliadic' Aeneid

Aeneid VI is the pivot of the whole poem. It is the transition from the 'Odyssean' to the 'Iliadic' Aeneid, as it is Aeneas' personal transition from the role of wanderer to that of *dux* (commander, leader), from exile and near-despair (as articulated in his speech during the storm, when he wishes he had died at Troy) to a sense of mission and responsibility, the result of his meeting with his father in the underworld. His mission is first revealed to him by the Sibyl, who warns him that he will have to fight to secure his right to settle and found a dynasty in Italy, then by the shade of Anchises, who shows him the as yet unborn heroes of the Rome which is to be, the Romans whose line he will inaugurate when he marries Lavinia, daughter of the king of the Latins. Anchises' prophecy addresses not only his son, but the Roman of the poet's own day: 'remember, Roman, your task is to rule, to establish peace and civilisation, to put down the proud and spare the defeated'.

For Aeneas, the Sibyl's prophecy that he must fight a war in Latium is of more immediate concern than the grand unfolding of the distant future by Anchises, a commentary addressed, as it were, over his son's head to generations yet unborn, the readers of the poem itself. Aeneas' present task is that to which the Sibyl alerts him:

> bella, horrida bella,
> et Thybrim multo spumantem sanguine cerno.
> nec Simois tibi ne Xanthus nec Dorica castra
> defuerint; alius Latio iam partus Achilles,
> natus et ipse dea . . .
> causa mali tanti coniunx iterum hospita Teucris
> externique iterum thalami.
> VI. 86–94
> War, dreadful war,
> And the river Tiber foaming with blood. This I see.
> You shall have your Simois, your Xanthus, your Greek camp,
> And another Achilles already awaits you in Latium,
> He too the son of a goddess . . .
> And the cause of all this misery to you Trojans
> Is once more a foreign marriage and a foreign bride.

All the references here are to the *Iliad*. The rivers Simois and Xanthus in Troy will reappear as the Tiber, the Latin camp will replace the Greek one, the second Achilles who awaits Aeneas is Turnus, like Aeneas and Achilles the son of a goddess. The 'cause of all this misery' is Lavinia, betrothed to Turnus until Aeneas' arrival caused her father King Latinus to change his mind, seeing in Aeneas the foreign prince promised by the oracles. Thus the roles are already being distributed for a 're-run' of the *Iliad*, with Lavinia as Helen, wife of Menelaus, taken by Paris. But just as the story of Helen is not the principal theme of the *Iliad*, the story of Lavinia is not the principal theme of the *Aeneid*. Homer's principal theme was the wrath of Achilles, his quarrel with

Agamemnon the Greek commander-in-chief, his withdrawal in pique from the war, and the dire consequences of that withdrawal to the Greeks. The Trojan champion Hector killed Achilles' friend Patroclus who went into battle wearing the armour of Achilles. Patroclus' death brought Achilles back into action, and his killing of Hector forms the climax of the *Iliad*.

The events of the *Iliad* form, as it were, the 'sub-text' of the second half of the *Aeneid*. Virgil himself signals early in book VII that a greater matter is to be his new theme, the theme of war:

> dicam horrida bella,
> dicam acies actosque animis in funera reges,
> Tyrrhenamque manum totamque sub arma coactam
> Hesperiam. maior rerum mihi nascitur ordo,
> maius opus moueo.
> VII. 41–45
> I shall tell of dreadful war,
> Of the battlefield and great Kings driven by their courage to death,
> Of the army of Etruria, all Italy under arms.
> For me there begins a greater order of things,
> I start a greater work.

The 'greater work' is a reference to the *Iliad*, regarded in antiquity as greater than the more genial and relaxed *Odyssey*, for it dealt with the tragic theme of war. Virgil's words '*dicam horrida bella*' are an echo of the words of the Sibyl to Aeneas in book VI. As for the 'greater order of things', this recalls the fourth eclogue (see above, pp. 14–15) which prophesied the renewal of a golden age, but only after further warfare:

> erunt etiam altera bella,
> atque iterum ad Troiam magnus mittetur Achilles.
> wars will occur again,
> and once again great Achilles will be drafted to Troy.

The ancients were familiar with a 'cyclic' view of history in which patterns of events are repeated. But Virgil also felt that with the coming of Augustus the recurring cycle of evil and good would be broken and that, with the defeat of Antony and Cleopatra, a more permanent peace might ensue. The victory

Aeneas must secure in that remote bronze-age Italy was the necessary first step towards that ultimate peace: the replication of the Trojan war leading this time to a Trojan victory. Aeneas arrives in Latium on a mission of peace: he wishes only to found a settlement for his exiled Trojans. This arrival is the first of Virgil's significant modifications of Homer. This is no expeditionary force, and the war which Aeneas is forced into is not of his seeking: it is caused by Turnus, who is angry at being rejected as a suitor in favour of the new-comer. Aeneas is forced to seek allies and goes to visit an old friend of his father's, the Greek prince Evander who left his native Arcadia to settle beside the Tiber on the site of the future Rome. Evander entrusts his young son Pallas to Aeneas' protection. In the ensuing war Turnus kills Pallas, who thus assumes the role of Patroclus in Virgil's 'Iliad': the killing of Turnus by Aeneas forms the climax of the *Aeneid* as the killing of Hector by Achilles had formed the climax of the *Iliad*.

Aeneas also enlists the support of the Etruscan King Tarchon, and it is while he is absent on these diplomatic missions that the war starts and goes badly for the Trojans, just as during Achilles' absence in the *Iliad* the war had gone badly for the Greeks. But Aeneas is not absent out of pique, anger or hurt pride: again, Virgil has transformed the old Homeric heroic code into something new and wholly Roman. The motive which brings Achilles back into the war is revenge against Hector for killing Patroclus. When Aeneas returns to the war at the head of his Etruscan allies, Pallas has not yet been killed by Turnus. Although Aeneas, to his bitter regret, cannot prevent Pallas' death, he throws himself into the fight with renewed vigour, killing the renegade ex-leader of the Etruscans, the dispossessed tyrant Mezentius, and also his young son, an act which might indeed seem to be one of revenge for Pallas' death. But Aeneas had been *in loco parentis* to Pallas, his father had entrusted him to his tutelage, so that he feels a debt to Evander which must be repaid in the final killing of Turnus. It is thus true to say that personal motives as well as dynastic ones do enter into his actions. Nor is Aeneas without anger: indeed, *furor*, the madness of war, dominates the last four books of the *Aeneid* and permeates Aeneas' actions on the battlefield no less than it does those of his opponents. But the element of pique has been removed. Homeric heroes fought for their own personal glory; there was little sense of collective patriotism and even less of divine mission. Throughout the Iliadic *Aeneid*, the reader is conscious of the goal for which all the bloodshed is taking place: not the destruction of a city but its eventual founding. In many passages in the last four books, Virgil directly imitates Homer: in the individual acts of prowess (*aristeia*) of each hero, in the similes which accompany the descriptions, in the unsparing record of the victims of war. Virgil takes much further the sympathy expressed by Homer, a Greek poet, for the doomed Trojan Hector: great artists are not narrowly partisan, and the ultimate fall of Troy is viewed sadly by Homer, not gloatingly. Virgil expresses a profound empathy for the young men on both sides who are war's victims.

Youth was not a notable feature of Homer's warriors who had all been fighting for ten years when the poem opens, whereas many of the young men who fought in Latium were untried warriors, in action for the first time, like some of those in the First World War; and indeed, in many of his descriptions of fighting Virgil draws close to the spirit of Wilfred Owen and the pity of war, while in no way reducing the epic grandeur of individual heroic prowess. Thus in book IX the *aristeia* of the young Trojan heroes Nisus and Euryalus, who are killed on a mission to recall Aeneas to the battlefield, are treated Homerically; but their mutual affection and self-sacrificing deaths draw from Virgil some of his most personal and empathising verses.

Chapter 3

Reading the *Aeneid*

10 The text

The modern reader of the *Aeneid*, whether he reads it in Latin or in translation, will be reading a text which, in its physical appearance, seems no different from, say, a text of *Paradise Lost*. Nevertheless, it is worth reflecting briefly on the differences between an ancient and a modern text. Ancient texts were written on scrolls or rolls: long 'books' like the twelve into which the *Aeneid* is divided, each of between 700 and 1,000 lines, would take up one roll each: the number of the 'book' would be inscribed on the end of the roll, such divisions facilitating the location of particular works or passages in large public or private collections. The Alexandrian age (third to second centuries BC) was the age of the first great public libraries, and by Virgil's time wealthy and cultivated men possessed their own libraries. Augustus founded two public libraries in Rome, to which later emperors added.

The modern form of the book, with sewn gatherings (the 'codex'), came in with the Christian era, and all surviving complete manuscripts of classical authors are 'codices', since none is earlier than the fourth century AD; we need not consider here the large number of papyrus fragments of Greek writers which survive from the second and third centuries BC. The earliest surviving manuscripts of the *Aeneid* date from the fourth century AD and are magnificently inscribed in capital letters, often with ornamentation: the ancient equivalent of deluxe editions. They reflect the immense reputation of the poem during the centuries following Virgil's death, when it became a textbook in the schools of grammar and rhetoric, and the subject of the first exhaustive commentaries on any ancient work. These early manuscripts

reflect a remarkably sound and authentic text, which goes
back through lost intermediaries to the poet's own autograph.
There are, naturally, many disputed and alternative readings,
but generally speaking the modern reader need not doubt that
he has what Virgil wrote. The earliest attempts to establish the
text go back to the poem's first editors, and throughout its
two thousand years of life it has been subjected to continuous
scrutiny, refinement and emendation as the techniques of tex-
tual and critical analysis have developed, so that today our
understanding of the poem is probably more complete than
at any previous time; though, as is the case with all literary
landmarks, each generation reads and interprets it in accordance with its own *zeitgeist*.

One feature of the text, briefly mentioned above (p. 10)
needs further emphasis here, since it is only apparent to those
who read the poem in Latin; the various English translators
do not attempt to reproduce it. When Virgil died he left the
poem complete but unrevised, and the presence in the text of
nearly sixty unfinished lines (hemistichs) confirms this
unrevised state. No other Latin hexameter poem contains any
imperfect hexameters, and though some of those in the
Aeneid may seem highly effective to a modern sensibility,
brought up on deliberately fragmentary discourses like *The
Waste Land*, ancient poets did not share our romantic affection for the irregular, the abandoned, or the incomplete: their
aim was always to offer a composition as highly finished as
possible. It seems certain that Virgil would have revised the
passages in which these hemistichs occur had he lived. Their
presence in the poem is explained by the account given in the
ancient *Life* of the poet's method of composition. First he
wrote a prose draft, then began to compose verses in blocks,
not necessarily in order, leaving certain lines unfinished so as
not to hold up the flow of composition. He called these unfinished lines *tibicines* (props) because they supported the
structure until the final *columnae* (pillars) should be placed in
position. Many of the hemistichs occur at the beginning or
end of a paragraph, and confirm the poet's paragraphic mode
of composition. In particular, paragraphs of about thirty

lines are frequent, and two key passages, Jupiter's and Tiberinus' prophecies in books I and VIII, are in fact exactly thirty lines long.

11 The story

The *Aeneid* is a *carmen perpetuum*: not a poem which lasts forever, but a continuous or (to use a musical term) 'through-composed' work. It is, however, divided into twelve 'books', each of which articulates a movement in the narrative whole. Larger divisions are also apparent: we have seen that the poet himself planned his epic in two linked parts (see above, pp. 27–8), while the whole may also be seen as consisting of four 'triads' of three books each, with major climaxes placed at the end of books IV, VIII and XII, or, again, as six pairs of books, each even-numbered book containing a major episode or climax. A brief summary of the sequence is as follows:

I   After an opening 'proemium' or statement of theme, with an invocation to the Muse, we are introduced to Aeneas. He is trying to cross the Mediterranean on his way to Italy from Troy, when Juno, ever hostile to the Trojans, raises a storm with the aid of Aeolus, god of the winds. Neptune (Poseidon), angry at Juno's invasion of his prerogative, calms the storm, and Aeneas is cast ashore on the north African coast, with only seven of his original fleet of twenty ships still intact. His mother, the goddess Venus, Juno's rival, appeals to Jupiter to end Aeneas' sufferings; in reply, Jupiter prophesies not only that Aeneas will make safe landfall in Italy and establish a settlement, but also, looking far into the 'future', that from that first settlement will spring the mighty Roman race, culminating in Augustus Caesar. Venus then appears to Aeneas in disguise, and tells him that he has landed in Carthage; she relates the story of Dido, herself an exile and a widow, who is trying to found a new settlement just as Aeneas must do. Aeneas, protected and concealed by a mist in which Venus has enveloped him, proceeds inland and sees the Tyrians building the new Carthage; in the temple which is being built in honour of Juno — significantly, the anti-Trojan goddess is worshipped by the city which will one day, under Hannibal, be Rome's greatest enemy – scenes from the Trojan war are depicted, by which Aeneas is deeply moved, especially since he himself is included in the pictures: his fame has got to Carthage before him. Dido appears; Aeneas introduces himself, the mist having now dispersed, and she escorts him to her palace where a feast is set. Meanwhile, Venus arranges that Cupid shall substitute himself for Aeneas' son Ascanius and, so disguised, bring gifts to Dido; Dido falls in love with Aeneas through his supposed child, and, wishing to prolong the evening, invites him to tell the story of his wanderings.

II   Aeneas recalls for Dido the last night of Troy, starting with the stratagem of the wooden horse by which the Greeks infiltrated and sacked the city, killing the King, Priam. He tells of his own escape, with his wife and son and the household gods of Troy, and of how his wife disappeared; he returned to the city to search for her; her image appeared to him, foretelling his safe arrival in a western land and asking him not to grieve for her.

III   Aeneas continues his narrative to Dido, describing his journey from Troy to north Africa via Crete and Sicily. Several of his adventures are closely modelled on those of Homer's Odysseus. The narrative ends with the death of Aeneas' father Anchises; wifeless and fatherless, with his small son to protect, Aeneas must now go forward to his destiny in Italy – a destiny in which Dido can have no place.

IV   Dido's passion for Aeneas has grown during his narrative; now it gets out of control; Aeneas returns her love, but when Mercury, the messenger of the gods, appears to him to remind him of his destiny, he sails away. Dido, distraught, curses his race and kills herself.

V   The Trojans, once more on the high seas, encounter another storm and put ashore in Sicily, where Aeneas honours the anniversary of his father's death with funeral games (modelled on those in *Iliad* XXIII). Juno sends Iris down from Olympus to incite the Trojan women to burn the ships; the women, tired of exile, set the ships on fire, but

Jupiter quenches the flames with a thunderstorm and only four ships are destroyed. Aeneas is persuaded to leave behind those of his comrades who have lost their ships or their will to continue; the rest set sail again for Italy. Anchises appears to Aeneas in his sleep and tells him to visit the Sibyl, prophetess of Cumae, who will guide him to the underworld, there to learn the full greatness of the Roman mission. Neptune promises Venus that the Trojans will cross safely to Italy but exacts as his price one innocent victim, the helmsman Palinurus.

VI   Aeneas and his small band of remaining comrades land at Cumae on the gulf of Naples, where, as instructed by his father's shade, he visits the underworld, guided by the prophetess, the Sibyl of Cumae, who tells him that he must fight a war to survive in Italy; she conducts him to the Elysian fields, where the shade of his father reveals to him the future lineage of Roman heroes, culminating in Augustus, but with a sad postscript: the early death is 'foretold' of Augustus' heir-designate, Marcellus, who died while Virgil was writing the *Aeneid*.

VII   Aeneas sails round the coast to the mouth of the Tiber. Virgil now invokes the Muse afresh for the second and greater part of his epic (above, pp. 32–3) and describes the situation in Latium: its elderly ruler, Latinus, has been told by the oracle that his daughter Lavinia, whom Turnus, chief of the Rutuli, seeks in marriage, is destined to marry a foreign chief whose descendants will rule not only Latium but the world. Aeneas sends ambassadors to King Latinus, who receives them hospitably, hails Aeneas as the foreign husband of whom the oracles have spoken, and promises alliance. Juno, having failed to prevent Aeneas' safe arrival in Italy, seeks to thwart him by sending the Fury Allecto to stir up strife in Italy. Latinus' queen, Amata, sides with Turnus, who is roused by Allecto to take up arms. Latinus refuses to fight, and, unable to control Turnus and his people, retires to his palace and lets events take their course. A muster of the Italian leaders, Aeneas' new enemies, parades before the reader; bringing up the rear are Turnus and the Amazonian figure of Camilla, leader of the Volsci.

VIII   In accordance with the Sibyl's promise that he would get help from an unlikely source, a Greek city, Aeneas proceeds up the Tiber to the very site of Rome, then supposed by Virgil to be inhabited by a colony of Arcadian exiles whose king, Evander, had known Anchises. Evander takes Aeneas on a guided tour of the sacred places of Rome's future history, and entrusts his son Pallas to Aeneas' protection. With these reinforcements Aeneas rides off to Caere to receive from Venus fresh armour, including a shield on which are depicted scenes from the future history of Rome, culminating in the battle of Actium and the triumph of Augustus.

IX   Aeneas seeks further allies in Etruria; during his absence the Italians attack the Trojan camp. Two Trojan heroes, Nisus and Euryalus, offer to try to reach Aeneas but are killed: theirs are the first examples in the *Aeneid* of the Homeric *aristeia*. Turnus enters the Trojan camp but is repulsed after a successful *aristeia* (the heroic exploits of individual combatants for personal glory) and rejoins his army by plunging into the Tiber.

X   Jupiter presides at a council of the gods and urges them to stop stirring up strife between the Latins and the Trojans, a civil conflict which he did not will. Venus and Juno argue angrily, but Jupiter declares his own impartiality and decrees that fate must now find the way; each hero must carve out his own destiny. Aeneas returns at the head of his Etruscan and Arcadian reinforcements; in the ensuing fighting, the fiercest in the poem, Pallas is killed by Turnus; in a furious *aristeia* not unlike that of Homer's Achilles, Aeneas kills Mezentius, one of the greatest of the Italian heroes, and his young son Lausus.

XI   A truce is called for the funeral of Pallas and the burial and burning of the dead of both sides. The Latins call a council of war. Drances, who hates Turnus, proposes that they should sue for peace, especially as an attempt to persuade the Greek veteran of Troy, Diomedes, who has settled in Italy, to join the war against his old foes has failed. Turnus angrily demands that they fight on, and offers, if all else fails, to face Aeneas in single combat. Meanwhile, the war is resumed and a spectacular cavalry engagement is led by Camilla, while Turnus attempts to ambush Aeneas. But the cavalry are routed, Camilla, after a brilliant *aristeia*, is killed, and Aeneas rides through to safety; the book ends with the Trojans on the offensive.

XII Faced with rout and probable defeat, Turnus agrees to meet Aeneas in single combat. There is a truce, which the Rutuli, persuaded by Turnus' sister Juturna, sacrilegiously break. Aeneas is wounded, and general fighting is resumed. In Olympus Jupiter and Juno resolve the conflict, Juno agreeing to give up her hostility to the Trojans on condition that the name of Troy will vanish from history and the united peoples be known as Italians. Meanwhile, Jupiter sends a Fury which terrifies Turnus; Juturna withdraws from the battle and he realises, like Faustus at the end of Marlowe's play, that he is quite alone: *di me terrent et Juppiter hostis*: 'the gods terrify me and Jupiter is my enemy'. In the final duel Aeneas has Turnus at his mercy, and might have spared him had he not recognised Pallas' sword-belt which Turnus had stripped from the young hero's body after he had slain him. Aeneas remembers his promise to Evander and plunges in the sword.

12 Structure

All great poets draw on, and modify, the work of their predecessors, and indeed what makes a poet great, and in the truest sense original, is precisely his 'esemplastic' power, to use Coleridge's term: his power to render into a new artefact the diverse elements, structural, thematic and linguistic, which he has found in the work of others. Of all European poets Virgil is perhaps the finest example of a writer who drew continually on the past, a learned writer ('doctus poeta'), who transformed the material of his reading into an authoritatively new discourse. In particular, as has been shown above (pp. 24–35) Virgil used and transformed Homer: his reworking of the plot of the *Iliad* to form the structure of *Aeneid* IX–XII is a most remarkable instance of what is nowadays called intertextuality — the reading of one text through another. This is something more significant than allusion or 'borrowing': it is a reassertion of the greatness of Homer in terms of a different language and a different civilisation. In the words of Jonathan Culler (*The Pursuit of Signs*) 'the meaning of a text depends upon other texts which it absorbs and transforms'.

The intertextuality of the *Aeneid* depends not only upon its structural and thematic recension of Homer, but also on an elaborate and complex system of allusion, correspondence and parallelism, drawing on Homer but also on Greek tragedy and philosophy, Hellenistic poetry, and earlier Latin writers, notably Ennius, Catullus and Lucretius, phrases and cadences from whose poetry are echoed and, as it were, reaffirmed by Virgil's authoritative reminiscence. The modern reader, brought up on another great poet of allusion, T. S. Eliot, should have little difficulty with this technique. Eliot himself paid homage, in *What is a Classic?*, to Virgil's uses of the past, and his unique status as the supreme voice of the consciousness of Rome and of the Latin language itself: the voice of a civilisation which had absorbed and transformed past civilisations, a transformation which the *Aeneid* itself enacts, and which is the poem's peculiar and unrepeatable achievement.

The fourth book of the *Aeneid* is a good example of the way Virgil transformed a Homeric motif by assimilating to it various post-Homeric elements. Dido's passionate and fatal love for Aeneas, whom she tries to detain from continuing on his destined journey to Rome, has its seed in the episode in the *Odyssey* in which Calypso detains Odysseus for a while but is then obliged, just as Dido is, by divine intervention to release him. The Homeric parting of these lovers is good-humoured, matter of fact and down-beat; after some initial tears and resistance, Calypso actually helps Odysseus on his way. Dido becomes distraught, denounces Aeneas in violent rhetoric, curses his descendants, and when he accedes to the will of the gods and sets sail, commits suicide. Virgil makes of this episode one of literature's great tragic romances. He used the story of Jason and Medea from the Hellenistic epic the *Argonautica*, by Apollonius of Rhodes, a tale also of violent passion, but this too he transcends. The intense empathy with which he treats Dido's ultimately uncontrollable passion goes far beyond the literary powers of Apollonius. When his Medea falls in love with Jason, Apollonius tells us that 'Cupid's arrow burns deep in her heart like flame'; but, as Sainte-Beuve remarked, his narrative 'does not make a single heart beat faster'. When Dido becomes aware of what she feels for Aeneas, she herself tells us, addressing her sister Anna in words whose dramatic force is closer to the spirit of Greek tragedy than to anything in earlier narrative poetry, and whose psychological insight looks forward rather than back:

> agnosco veteris vestigia flammae
> I recognise the traces of an ancient fire.

So the widow Dido, as Shakespeare calls her in *The Tempest*, falls in love again; her whole being is shaken. Cupid's arrow indeed burns in her heart, and in a celebrated simile she is compared to a deer hit by an arrow from a hunter who does not even realise that he has wounded her: that hunter, of course, is Aeneas, unaware of the violence of the flame he has reawakened. The first lines of book IV describe the queen's passion as an internal wound which she feeds in her veins, a kind of self-consuming fire. Images of fire and wounds recur through this book, operating as signifiers of a deadly trauma.

The structure of book IV is like that of a Greek tragedy, with scenes between the protagonists (Aeneas, Dido and her sister-confidante Anna), divine messengers and interventions, with the author as chorus, not only narrating but commenting on the action; on the 'marriage' between Dido and Aeneas symbolically enacted in a cave during a storm while the lovers are out hunting, the poet comments: 'She (Dido), being no longer moved by appearances or what people said, did not trouble to hide her love affair; she called it a marriage, using the word as a cover for her *culpa* or wrongdoing' (see below, section 14). But although book IV may be read as a separate story (just as book II, the fall of Troy, forms a self-contained story), it is nevertheless completely integrated into the structure of the work as a whole. The poem is about a dutiful hero who, albeit at first reluctantly, follows the gods' will through much suffering and labour to inaugurate a historical process which will culminate in the triumph of Augustus. The episode of Dido is a love story, and love is the antithesis of history, for it is timeless; it is the supreme anti-historical force, seeking to bring the forward progression of events to a halt or to initiate a different sequence of events altogether, dictated not by divine providence but by individual desire. The winter Aeneas spends with Dido is a period out of time, the Roman mission is suspended.

Dido cannot bear to return from her love to the world of political realities. When Aeneas leaves, she can see only one way: from the timeless ahistorical world of love to the timeless ahistorical world of death.

Although, as has been said, the *Aeneid* is a continuous or through-composed epic, it is constructed as a sequence of episodes which balance and interact with each other. The allusions, correspondences and parallels with earlier works are assimilated into a discourse of allusion and correspondence *within itself*, so that the poem is self-referential or, in the words of J. K. Newman (*The Classical Epic Tradition*) 'a continuous commentary on itself'. The reader is invited to make connections and to see correspondences between different parts of the text, to notice recurring *leitmotiv* as in a musical composition: the word *fatum*, fate, for example, is repeated some 120 times (see below, section 19). If there is a single organizing concept which controls the entire discourse, it is this concept of *fatum*.

Characters, themes and episodes from the two halves of the poem offer parallels and correspondences. Thus, in the Dido episode, the opening lines of book IV describe Dido's internal wound, the trauma festering within her. The opening of book XII describes Turnus' state of mind, violent and desperate, as he senses the battle drawing near to its end and realises that he must challenge Aeneas at last. He is compared to an

African lion (Dido was an African queen) wounded by a hunter, aroused by his own blood. Now Turnus is not actually wounded, and the simile of the lion and the hunter's arrow recalls not only Dido's psychological love-wound but also the simile, referred to above, of the queen as a wounded deer; her wound was inflicted, unawares, by Aeneas, and it is Aeneas whose continued evasion of Turnus' attacks has roused Turnus to fresh *furor*.

There are significant correspondences also between the proudly self-vaunting farewell speeches of Dido (book IV) and Turnus (book XII). Both are tragic figures, doomed by their own fault, both reach the end of their tether. Both speak to their sisters. Dido turns away to the funeral pyre on which she is about to immolate herself (like Wagner's Brünnhilde at the end of *Götterdämmerung*) and sadly apostrophises the things Aeneas had worn and left behind, intimate reminders of their time together:

> accipite hanc animam meque his exsolvite curis.
> vixi et quem dederat cursum Fortuna peregi,
> et nunc magna mei sub terras ibit imago.
> Receive this soul, release me from this pain.
> I have lived my life, finished the course Fortune allotted,
> And my great ghost shall now go down beneath the earth.
>
> (652–4)

Turnus, after confiding to his sister his realisation of imminent defeat, apostrophises the Manes, the spirits of the underworld, who will shortly receive his soul:

> vos o mihi, Manes,
> este boni, quoniam superis aversa voluntas.
> sancta ad vos anima atque istius inscia culpae
> descendam magnorum haud umquam indignus avorum.
> You spirits of the dead,
> Be kind to me, now that the gods above
> Favour me no more. A guiltless soul, my duty done,
> I shall go down, worthy of my great forbears.
>
> (646–9)

The Italian renaissance epic poet Tasso wrote a discourse on the heroic poem in which he classified the various episodes of the *Aeneid* into two categories: those which helped the

hero on his mission (*mezzi* or instruments) and those which
hindered him (*impedimenti*). Dido in the first half of the
poem and Turnus in the second constitute Aeneas' greatest
impediments: the parallel between them is again pointed by
Turnus' refusal to admit any guilt; so too, Dido cloaked her
culpa under the pretext of marriage. At whatever personal
cost — he weeps when preparing to leave Dido, he hesitates
before killing Turnus — Aeneas must overcome these impediments. The contrast between instruments and impediments
occurs throughout the poem, and is secured by the reader
when he makes connections between images and symbols in
different parts of the text. Thus Dido leads Aeneas into her
splendid and luxurious palace, while in book VIII Evander,
an aged and impoverished Greek immigrant who presides
over a primitive settlement on the site of Rome, welcomes
Aeneas into his simple rustic dwelling on the Palatine hill,
imagined by the poet to stand on the very site of what was to
be Augustus' own house. This contrast polarises the poem's
entire moral structure: 'oriental' luxury belongs to the past,
to the fallen palace of Priam, renowned in the *Iliad* for its
splendour, and to Dido's doomed Carthage, while *Roma
aeterna* and its *imperium sine fine*, the eternal city and its
empire without end, grew from simple pastoral origins —
Evander's hut, Romulus' cave.

Virgil's vision of Roman history forms the central organizing principal of the *Aeneid* and provides the clearest example
of a planned parallelism. Structurally, the description in book
VI of the great men who will build the glory of Rome, in the
form of souls awaiting rebirth in Elysium identified by
Anchises for Aeneas, is paralleled by the description in book
VIII of the Shield made for Aeneas by Vulcan at Venus'
instigation, on which are depicted scenes from the future
history of Rome, from Romulus to Augustus. Both these
episodes must be read with the first book of the poem in
mind: the reader is expected to recall Jupiter's first speech, in
which he reassures Venus that Aeneas will reach Italy safely
and inaugurate the 'future' of Rome. All three of these
passages contain praise of the exploits of Augustus Caesar.

A final point must be made about the structure of the poem as a whole. In common with other ancient works of great length, most significantly and remarkably the *Iliad*, the *Aeneid* is an example of 'ring-composition', a structural technique in which the close of a work recalls and mirrors its opening. Thus the *Iliad* begins with Achilles refusing to give back the girl Briseis, and with an assembly of the gods which supports his refusal. At the end of the poem, Achilles voluntarily gives back the body of Hector to Priam, accepting from Priam the ransom he refused to accept from Agamemnon. The gods themselves require this action from him, and the book thus ends with a resolution of the 'wrath' which has permeated the poem. In the *Aeneid*, the first book shows us Aeneas frightened, shipwrecked, shivering with cold and expecting death by drowning. In the episode on Olympus already referred to, Jupiter reassures the hero's anxious mother, Venus, that Aeneas will survive. In book XII, it is Turnus whose limbs dissolve in the cold of death: the same phrase, *solvuntur frigore membra*, is used here as was used of Aeneas in book I. Jupiter's speech to Venus in book I is balanced by a speech to Juno in book XII. In book I Juno's hatred stirred up the storm in which Aeneas nearly perished, in book VII her hatred stirred up the war in Latium, but now she agrees to be reconciled to the Trojans provided they drop the hated name forever and become Italians and Romans. Again, the predetermined course of history is asserted in terms of a pretended 'prophecy' and the poem, which started with Aeneas near to despair and death, ends with his victory over Turnus. In book I, if Aeneas had continued to suffer as Juno intended, that would have been the end: *et iam finis erat*, writes the poet, 'that was the end of that', as the hero and his few surviving comrades huddle miserably on the alien shore of Africa. A routine transitional formula of epic narrative – but then comes the scene on Olympus when Jupiter reassures Venus, the hero's mother, that all shall be well despite Juno's opposition to destiny. *quem das finem, rex magne, laborum?* 'What end do you give, great King, to his labours?' asks Venus anxiously, thus eliciting the first of

the poem's great prophetic set-pieces about Rome, and
(again) recalling in the reader's memory Aeneas' words of en-
couragement to his suffering men in book I: *deus dabit his
quoque finem*, 'to this also god will grant an end'.

The theme of the end is thus a powerful motif at the beginning of the poem, and is echoed in book XII when Jupiter
asks Juno *'quae iam finis erit, coniunx?* 'What is to be the
end [of this hostility of yours]?' Jupiter at this point decides
'the end' which is also the end of the poem and, as promised
in book I, of Aeneas' labours. When he wins Juno's final
consent, Jupiter *smiles* in agreement to her supposed 'condition' that the name of Trojan shall vanish into the past;
smiles, because the goddess who has personified an almost
satanic opposition to the divine will is at last in consonance
with it. And that smile is the same smile with which, the poet
tells us, Jupiter reassured Venus in book I when he first
unrolled the book of destiny. In that repeated phrase, *olli
subridens*, 'smiling on her', Virgil spans and overarches the
entire *Aeneid*, which is enacted as narrative inside those two
Olympian dialogues. The narrative is like all epic narrative,
moving forward in time to a destined 'end', but it is also
cyclic, for the end is foreseen in the beginning and the beginning recalled at the end. The poem's narrative time must also
be related to history itself: 'past', 'present' and 'future' form
two different sets of coordinates, one inside the poem, the
other in the perspective of the reader. The structure of the
Aeneid is thus simultaneously diachronic (moving through
narrative time) and synchronic (a stasis in which a Homeric
hero, Augustus and events and characters in between, are
presented in the simultaneity of a single discourse).

Ancient historians saw history as a series of 'cycles', a
structure of recurring patterns. In the *Aeneid* certain themes
and 'types' recur, as for Virgil they did in history itself. The
impediments in the poem are not merely those opposed
to Aeneas: before his coming, we are told in book VIII,
Hercules came to the site of Rome, and freed its earliest
inhabitants from the monster Cacus who haunted the
Aventine hill. And long after Aeneas, in the culmination of

a cyclic sequence, Augustus defeated Antony and Cleopatra and again (to put it flatteringly) saved Rome for civilisation. Aeneas' defeat of Turnus then takes its place in a recurring cycle of good versus evil and as a Homeric prelude to the poem's teleological Augustan climax, beyond which Virgil could not and did not look.

Can we then, or should we, read the *Aeneid* as an allegory? The author of the ancient *Life* of Virgil (see above, p. 24) observed that the poem was a structural and thematic reworking of Homer's epics which also included an account of the origins of Rome and Augustus. Virgil did not allegorize Augustus in his Aeneas; his special achievement lay rather in connecting legend with history through a synchronic structure. Aeneas is a type or prefiguration of Augustus, his deeds and labours (*facta et labores*), like those of his great predecessor Hercules, forming a paradigm of the achievements of the *princeps*. The Roman saw history as a series of models or *exempla*, to be followed by successive generations: hence the presentation of history in terms of recurrent cycles; and it is the exemplary conduct of Aeneas, his *pietas* and his prowess at war, which inspired the poet to see in his legend a way of transforming Roman annalistic chronicle into Homeric epic.

13 Expression and sensibility

Most of what has been said about the *Aeneid* hitherto may be apprehended by those who read the poem in translation. Themes, structural patterns, echoes of Homer, do not demand an ability to read Latin before they can be detected; images and similes can be translated; narrative episodes can be followed as effectively in English as in the original. But Virgil's style, the texture, sonorities and rhythms of his discourse, presents certain difficulties to the translator, which are not found in the rapid, concrete, repetitive and highly formalised discourse of Homer. Virgil's literary technique was already highly polished and sophisticated by the time he completed the *Georgics*, which stands as 'the most perfectly finished work, along with Horace's *Odes*, in the Latin language' (R. D. Williams). In the *Aeneid*, unrevised though it remained when he died, his technique became bolder and more advanced; he introduced a greater variety of tone, pace and rhythm; he took liberties with the Latin language, with the Latin hexameter and with the interaction of the flow of discourse (the 'sense') with the metrical unit (the 'line' or 'verse') which none of his successors was able to match. In the *Eclogues* the metrical unit (the line) and the sense-unit (the sentence) are kept in close correspondence, so that there is comparatively little enjambment or running-on of the sense-unit from one line to the next; in the *Eclogues*, too, there is relatively little elision; while in the *Aeneid*, especially in the later books, there is much enjambment, with many lines ending in weak words such as prepositions or conjunctions, and elision is more freely admitted.

Here is a short passage from book XII which includes both narrative and direct speech. First in Latin (elided syllables are in brackets):

> hunc procul ut campo Turnus prospexit aperto,
> ante levi iaculo longum per inane secutus
> sistit equos biiugis et curru desilit atque
> semianimi lapsoque supervenit, et pede collo
> impresso dextrae mucro (nem) extorquet et alto
> fulgentem tingit iugul (o at) qu(e) haec insuper addit:
> 'en agros et, quam bello, Troiane, petisti,
> Hesperiam metire iacens: haec praemia, qui me
> ferr (o) ausi temptare, ferunt, sic moenia condunt.'
>
> (XII.353–61)

Now in the classic English version, that of Dryden (1697):

> Fierce Turnus viewed the Trojan from afar,
> And launched his javelin from his lofty car,
> Then lightly leaping down, pursued the blow,
> And pressing with his foot his prostrate foe,
> Wrenched from his feeble hold the shining sword,
> And plunged it in the bosom of its lord.
> 'Possess' (said he) 'the fruit of all thy pains,
> And measure, at thy length, our Latian plains.
> Thus are my foes rewarded, by my hand;
> Thus may they build their town, and thus enjoy the land!'

Now in a modern version, that of C. Day Lewis (1954):

> Well, Turnus noticed Eumedes far off on the open plain,
> And hitting him first with a long-range javelin drove over,
> Pulled up his pair of horses, leapt down from the chariot,
>   straddled
> The fallen, dying man, and putting his foot hard down
> On his neck, twisted the sword out of his hand, to plunge its
> Glittering blade deep into his throat; then spoke these words:
> 'Lie there, measure out with your length, you Trojan, the land
>   of Hesperia
> You wanted to grab by aggression. This is the pay-off
>   they get
> Who dare to take arms against me: thus do they found their
>   city.'

This passage contains relatively few elisions (only three). The first two lines are each 'self-contained'; that is, each line includes all the words necessary to make a sense-unit. Both translators are able to reflect this in their versions. The third line ends with the word 'and'. Shakespeare in his late plays sometimes admits this very bold enjambment:

> These our actors,
> As I foretold you, were all spirits, and
> Are melted into air, into thin air.
>
> (The Tempest 4.1.148–50)

Virgil's enjambment is ignored by Dryden, who uses end-stopped rhyming couplets in accordance with the fashion of his time. Day Lewis has enjambment, but ends the line with a 'strong' word ('straddled'). Virgil continues enjambment right through to the end of the sixth line. Again, Day Lewis attempts to reflect this continuity, but ends one line with 'its', which seems awkward in English. The three lines of direct speech contain in the Latin only one major sense break, in the middle of the middle line. Again, Day Lewis tries to keep this; Dryden ignores it. Another characteristic feature of Virgil's discourse is its paratactic structure: that is, he prefers to link sentences with 'and' rather than use subordinate clauses. There are six words meaning 'and' in the Latin (et . . . atque . . . et . . . et . . . atque . . . et). Here Dryden sustains the Virgilian flow better than Day Lewis, with five 'ands' and

a 'then' which works as a connective rather like 'and'. Day
Lewis prefers to link his sentences by asyndeton: that is to
say, the omission of the copulative ('drove over, pulled up,
leapt down').

Another feature of Virgil's poetry which may not always be
easy to render in translation is his fondness, shared with other
Latin poets, for alliteration. This is not because English
poetry does not alliterate; on the contrary, it has been a
marked feature of our verse since Anglo-Saxon times, and,
indeed, certain later poets, notably Tennyson, consciously try
to capture Latin alliterative effects ('the murmur of in-
numerable bees'). No problem arises when English words can
be found to reproduce the alliterative pattern of the Latin. In
the phrase of Tennyson, *murmur* is itself a Latin word and in-
numerable is the Latin *innumerabilis*. Sometimes, however,
the alliterative pattern cannot be reproduced. In the passage
from *Aeneid* XII, the first line contains five p- sounds. Day
Lewis has two, Dryden none. And in the last line, alliteration
of m- is sustained from the previous line and alliteration of
f- is combined with another feature of Latin poetry of which
Virgil is particularly fond: word-play, assonance of two
words with similar sounds but different meanings, such
assonance often ignoring 'quantity' (length of syllable): *ferro*
('sword') here chimes with *ferunt* ('take away'). Dryden
cleverly repeats the word 'thus' and extends the verse into an
alexandrine, which helps to reproduce the epigrammatic effect of the last line of the speech in the original. Day Lewis'
version is closer in sense to the Latin (though 'pay-off' is an
inappropriate piece of modern slang) but does not retain the
alliteration or the word-play.

The passage just considered was *not* a 'highlight', but a
representative piece of narrative chosen more or less at ran-
dom. Some of the more famous passages of the poem may
now be considered in order to illustrate further Virgil's extraordinary sensitivity to language. One of the most remarkable features of the *Aeneid* is the way in which Virgil man-
aged to combine the old Roman grandeur of Ennius and
Lucretius and the scope and sweep of Homeric narrative

with an altogether different kind of literary sensibility influenced by the Alexandrian poets of the Hellenistic era and their Latin admirers, the so called *neoteroi* ('new poets'), notably Catullus: these writers, as has been said above, turned away from the monumental, preferring the lyrical, the subjective and the personal. The achievement of Augustan poetry, and especially of Virgil, lay in 'purifying the dialect of the tribe' (to quote T. S. Eliot) until it became an instrument capable of the most subtle as well as the most powerful effects.

Here is part of Aeneas' funeral address over the body of Pallas, son of Evander, killed by Turnus:

> non haec Euandro de te promissa parenti
> discedens dederam, cum me complexus euntem
> mitteret in magn(um) imperium metuensque moneret
> acris esse viros, cum dura proelia gente.
> et nunc ille quidem spe multum captus inani
> fors et vota facit cumulatque altaria donis,
> nos iuven(em) exanim(um) et nil iam caelestibus ullis
> debentem vano maesti comitamur honore.
> infelix, nati funus crudele videbis.
> hi nostri reditus expectatique triumphi?

(XI.45–54)

To gain the full effect of this deeply emotional passage it should be read aloud. (Elided syllables are in brackets and alliterations and assonances underlined.) The preponderance of long vowels and syllables is striking. The Latin hexameter consists of six feet, most of which can be either dactyls (-vv) or spondees (- -). Here spondees predominate, which slows the passage down to the mood and tempo of a funeral.

Here is a modern version, this time by Allen Mandelbaum (1970):

> For this was not the promise that I gave
> Evander when I left with his embrace,
> when he sent me to win a mighty empire,
> when he warned me, in fear, that I should meet
> men harsh in battle and a sturdy race,
> And even now, beguiled by empty hopes,
> perhaps Evander makes his vows and heaps
> his gifts upon the altar stone; while we

grieving, accompany the lifeless youth
who now owes nothing to the gods, although
we pay him useless honours. Luckless father,
you are to see your own son's funeral.
Is this our coming back, the victory
that we expected?

This translation renders well the slow measured pace of
the Latin and the simple pathos of the contrast between the
dead youth and the old father, unaware as yet of what has
occurred, who may perhaps (*fors et*) be even now carrying out
religious observances. The alliterative effects are not available
in English, nor the 'pathetic' elisions of line 51, which seem to
'elide' Pallas wholly out of existence, nor the hollow empty
grandeur of *expectatique triumphi* ('and the long awaited
triumphs'), nor the assonances of the long Latin vowels
(*cae*lestibus, *mae*sti).

Long vowels and slow spondees predominate throughout
the first two hundred lines of book XI, an immense sym-
phonic adagio depicting Pallas' funeral cortege. They
predominate, too, in the mysterious opening lines of the descent into the underworld in book VI:

> ibant obscuri sola sub nocte per umbram
> perque domos Ditis vacuas et inania regna

(VI.268–9)

Dryden catches the effect very well, partly by keeping the
Latin derivative 'obscure' and the alliteration of ḍ:

> Obscure they went through dreary shades that led
> Along the waste dominions of the dead.

Assonance and elision are used to moving effect in a passage
later in book VI, when the souls of the dead are depicted
waiting and yearning to cross the river which separates the living from the dead:

> Stabant orantes primi transmittere cursum
> tendebantque manus rip(ae) ulterioris amore.

(VI.313–4)

No English version that I know really does justice to these
lines. Robert Fitzgerald's (1981) is perhaps the best, because
it is the simplest:

> There all stood begging to be first across
> And reached out longing hands to the far shore.

William Empson, in *Seven Types of Ambiguity*, drew attention to these lines: '*ulterioris*, the word of their banishment, is long, and so shows that they have been waiting a long time; and because the repeated vowel-sound (itself the moan of hopeless sorrow) in *oris amore* connects the two words and makes desire belong necessarily to the unattainable.' He might have added that the *or* sound echoes that in *orantes* in the previous line ('begging', 'praying') so that the theme of longing and sorrow is carried through both lines. The elision of the long diphthong -ae in *ripae*, coming before *ulterioris*, also adds − in some way less readily definable − to the pathos and mystery of the lines.

Pathos is at its most eloquent in a famous line spoken in book I by Aeneas, who is looking at engravings of the Trojan war in the temple of Juno in Carthage:

> sunt lacrimae rerum et mentem mortalia tangunt
>
> (I.462)

The beauty and melancholy of the line has given it, in R. G. Austin's words, a 'mysterious universality' which has been endlessly discussed. It is indeed difficult not to hear behind Aeneas' voice another voice, that of the 'implied author', to use the term coined by Wayne Booth (*The Rhetoric of Fiction*), bringing (to quote Matthew Arnold) 'the eternal note of sadness in'. It is interesting to discover that Dryden, who was more responsive to the political and public voice of the *Aeneid* as a Roman poem than to the more ambiguous and doubtful voice of the 'implied author', does not attempt to translate this line at all. Here is Day Lewis:

> Tears in the nature of things, hearts touched by
>   human transience.

This is good in so far as it retains an alliterative pattern, though Virgil uses a pattern of $\underset{\sim}{m}$ s as well as $\underset{\sim}{t}$ s; it mistranslates the objective genitive 'rerum': strictly we should read, rather, 'tears *for* the nature of things.' Day

Lewis's 'in' over-romanticises the sentiment by implying that the tears are inherent *in* mortality rather than prompted *by* it: yet it could be said that the Latin actually allows for this kind of flexibility and ambiguity, or at least does not discourage it, since if we weep *for* mortality it must be because there is *in* mortality something which elicits our tears.

This last example may serve as a reminder that the flexibility and ambiguity of Virgil's style is partly owing to the flexibility of the Latin language, which he exploited more boldly than any other poet. Because Latin is an inflected language, in which the 'case' of a noun (nominative, accusative, genitive, etc.) is signified by its ending and the adjective 'agrees' with the noun, the actual order of words is often quite different from what would be possible in English. A Latin sentence is often not lineal but circular, so that the order in which things are said is of rhetorical rather than sequential significance, and the sentence must be taken as a whole. This is difficult for those used to modern syntax: if Virgil wishes to describe two simultaneous actions he often seems to put the cart before the horse, but is not in fact doing so: a famous example at II.353 reads *moriamur et in media arma ruamus*: 'let us die and rush into battle'. J. P. Postgate wrote definitively on this point in 1908 ('Flaws in Classical Research', *Proceedings of the British Academy* vol. 3, 1909): 'Not only does the lineal habit hinder our sight of real connections between the distant members of a sentence, but it causes us to find imaginary bonds between adjacent ones.' Virgil often uses 'enclosing word order', e.g. *ut campo Turnus prospexit aperto*, where the adjective 'open' is separated from the noun 'plain' by the words 'Turnus saw'. Often the same word has to be taken with more than one other word; sometimes a word has to be 'understood', that is read as if it were there, though it is not. The various juxtapositions and separations between elements in a Virgilian sentence often encourage the possibility of alternative or multiple significances. Sometimes the word-order seems to be displaced by an extremely flexible use of 'and' (especially in the form of the suffix *-que* appended to the word which is to be linked): to give a simple example, *flent maesti mussantque patres* means 'the grieving elders weep and dither', but the 'lineal' reading of the sentence is 'weep the grieving and dither elders'. It is thus seldom possible to translate the *Aeneid* 'as one goes along'.

In composing the poem Virgil developed a 'periodic' structure in which the sense is extended and diffused through several lines in a series of sentences or 'cola' often arranged in sets of three, usually linked by the copulative but sometimes arranged in asyndeton ('I came, I saw, I conquered'). Very often a statement is repeated once or twice in a slightly varied or amplified form. This figure, which James Henry, in his eccentric but monumental commentary on the poem, labelled 'theme and variation(s)', is common in all rhetorical or elevated discourse, but Virgil's use of it is so frequent and conspicuous that it must be held to constitute a distinguishing feature of his epic style.

Because the *Aeneid* is composed both 'paratactically' and paragraphically, reading the poem becomes a cumulative experience; consequently it is not easy to illustrate fully this and the other features of Virgil's poetic technique described above, except through a fairly long passage. Moreover, the selection of a 'representative' passage raises difficulties; the tone, texture and treatment of the various episodes varies greatly, for 'variatio' is itself a rhetorical figure on which any long work must depend in order to sustain the reader's interest. The style of a speech will be different from the narrative style; speeches themselves will vary from the majestic pronouncements of Jupiter to the angry exchanges of rival deities Juno and Venus, or of rival leaders Drances and Turnus in book XI; narrative will vary from descriptions of fighting to lyrical passages like the story of Camilla's early pastoral life in book XI or the shadowy mysterious journey to the underworld in book VI.

Here is a celebrated passage from book IX: two young Trojans, Nisus and Euryalus, volunteer to break through the Italian lines to reach Aeneas, who is away on a diplomatic mission seeking allies, and in whose absence the Trojans are under siege. This passage presents their heroic last stand and

their death. Structurally and thematically the episode is based
on *Iliad* X (with some assimilated features of *Iliad* IX), but
whereas the Homeric counterparts of the two heroes survive,
Virgil gives the story a tragic ending, 'affording one of the
outstanding examples of pathos in the whole poem' (R. D.
Williams), in which the empathising sensibility of the implied
author permeates and controls the narrative:

> dixerat et toto conixus corpore ferrum   410
> conicit. hasta volans noctis diverberat umbras
> et venit aversi in tergum Sulmonis ibique
> frangitur, ac fisso transit praecordia ligno.
> volvitur ille vomens calidum de pectore flumen
> frigidus et longis singultibus ilia pulsat.   415
> diversi circumspiciunt. hoc acrior idem
> ecce aliud summa telum librabat ab aure.
> dum trepidant, it hasta Tago per tempus utrumque
> stridens traiectoque haesit tepefacta cerebro.
> saevit atrox Volcens nec teli conspicit usquam   420
> auctorem nec quo se ardens immittere possit.
> 'tu tamen interea calida mihi sanguine poenas
> persolves amborum' inquit: simul ense recluso
> ibat in Euryalum. tum vero exterritus, amens,
> conclamat Nisus nec se celare tenebris   425
> amplius aut tantum potuit perferre dolorem:
> 'me, me, adsum qui feci, in me convertite ferrum,
> o Rutuli! mea fraus omnis, nihil iste nec ausus
> nec potuit; caelum hoc et conscia sidera testor;
> tantum infelicem nimium dilexit amicum'.   430
> talia dicta dabat, sed viribus ensis adactus
> transabiit costas et candida pectora rumpit.
> volvitur Euryalus leto, pulchrosque per artus
> it cruor inque umeros cervix conlapsa recumbit:
> purpureus veluti cum flos succisus aratro   435
> languescit moriens, lassove papavera collo
> demisere caput pluvia cum forte gravantur.
> at Nisus ruit in medios solumque per omnis
> Volcentem petit, in solo Volcente moratur.
> quem circum glomerati hostes hinc comminus
>   atque hinc   440
> proturbant. instat non setius ac rotat ensem
> fulmineum, donec Rutuli clamantis in ore
> condidit adverso et moriens animam abstulit hosti.
> tum super exanimum sese proiecit amicum
> confossus, placidaque ibi demum morte quievit.   445

Fortunati ambo! si quid mea carmina possunt,
nulla dies umquam memori vos eximet aevo,
dum domus Aeneae Capitoli immobile saxum
accolet imperiumque pater Romanus habebit.

(IX.410–449)

The most conspicuous feature of the Latin is its directness and rapidity of narrative. In the description of the spear-cast with which the passage begins there is some notable enjambment: vv. 412, 416, 420 (and also 440) all end with weak or 'indifferent' words ('and there', 'he', 'anywhere', 'from this side and that'). The very first sentence 'turns' into the first foot of the second line, then stops: the effort of hurling the spear is enacted in the abruptness of *ferrum/conicit* – an effect further emphasised in the assonance *conixus conicit* and the alliteration of these words with *corpore*. In the next sentence, the wounding of Sulmo, there is much interlacing alliteration of f and v (frangitur, fisso, volvitur, vomens, flumen, frigidus). The passage also exhibits extreme pathos, especially in the words of Nisus (427–30): he takes all the blame on himself, and his first line, with its repeated *me, me, . . . me*, and its remarkable elisions of *m (e)adsum, fec(i)in me*, leads to the famous verse 'tant(um) infelicem nimium dilexit amicum', where the pathos is in the simplicity of the words ('only he loved his unlucky friend too much') combined with their studied yet artless-seeming patterning: *tantum* (only, just) goes with the whole sentence, yet its juxtaposition with *infelicem* seems to increase Nisus' ill-luck; similarly, *nimium* goes with *dilexit* yet also seems to reinforce the emphasis on *infelicem*. The line is also markedly spondaic: the three long syllables of *dilexit* chime with the speech-stress (di-<u>lex</u>-it), as also do the five long syllables of *tant(um) infelicem*.

This passage has also been widely admired for the pathos of its simile, partly derived from Homer, but modified and softened by allusion to some famous elegiac lines of Catullus. The final lines are remarkable also: here the poet intervenes in his own narrative, not as 'implied author' but in a direct reference to his own poetry (*mea carmina*) and its power to immortalise its subject: a theme common in lyric poetry (Horace, for instance, says his *Odes* will continue to be read as long as Roman power survives), but rare in heroic epic. Ovid ends his *Metamorphoses* with a similar claim for immortality, but like Horace's his claim is for his own art. Virgil wishes to emphasise the immortality of two friends whose heroic deaths also carry 'romantic' undertones of elegiac and even erotic verse. But the implication of the postscript − and the same might be said of Shakespeare's claims to immortalise his Friend in the Sonnets − is that only the power of poetry − *si quid mea carmina possunt* − can confer this kind of immortality. Homer had established this *topos* in the *Iliad*, where heroic song immortalises the deeds of great heroes and also their disgrace, as when Helen says in *Iliad* VI that Zeus 'set a vile destiny' on her and Paris, 'so that hereafter we shall be made into things of song for the men of the future'. Homer makes Helen foresee her role in the *Iliad*, which we, and the poet, pretend to be as yet uncomposed. Virgil claims immortality for his two heroes through his own song, already composed and placed on record. This is the most personal and direct statement in the *Aeneid*, placed as the epilogue to a passage in which the empathising voice of the implied author is conspicuous throughout: especially in the treatment of the two heroes' deaths. A little earlier in the episode (IX.401) Nisus contemplated a suicide charge which would end in what Virgil calls *pulchra mors*, 'a lovely death': the phrase, and the romanticising flower-simile, have suggested to some critics that Virgil is idealising death; the effect is perhaps not unlike that of some of Wilfred Owen's verses:

> As bronze may be much beautified
> By lying in the dark damp soil,
> So men who fade in dust of warfare fade
> Fairer, and sorrow blooms their soul.

Here now are two English versions of this passage. First, Dryden's:

> Then from his ear
> He pois'd, and aim'd, and launch'd the trembling spear.

The deadly weapon, hissing from the grove,
Impetuous on the back of Sulmo drove;
Pierc'd his thin armor, drank his vital blood,
And in his body left the broken wood.
He staggers round; his eyeballs roll in death,
And with short sobs he gasps away his breath.
All stand amaz'd — a second jav'lin flies
With equal strength, and quivers thro' the skies.
This thro' thy temples, Tagus, forc'd the way,
And in the brainpan warmly buried lay.
Fierce Volscens foams with rage, and, gazing round,
Descried not him who gave the fatal wound,
Nor knew to fix revenge: 'But thou,' he cries,
'Shalt pay for both,' and at the pris'ner flies
With his drawn sword. Then, struck with deep despair,
That cruel sight the lover could not bear;
But from his covert rush'd in open view,
And sent his voice before him as he flew:
'Me! me!' he cried — 'turn all your swords alone
On me — the fact confess'd, the fault my own.
He neither could nor durst, the guiltless youth:
Ye moon and stars, bear witness to the truth!
His only crime (if friendship can offend)
Is too much love to his unhappy friend.'
Too late he speaks: the sword, which fury guides,
Driv'n with full force, had piec'd his tender sides.
Down fell the beauteous youth: the yawning wound
Gush'd out a purple stream, and stain'd the ground.
His snowy neck reclines upon his breast,
Like a fair flow'r by the keen share oppress'd;
Like a white poppy sinking on the plain,
Whose heavy head is overcharg'd with rain.
Despair, and rage, and vengeance justly vow'd,
Drove Nisus headlong on the hostile crowd.
Volscens he seeks; on him alone he bends:
Borne back and bor'd by his surrounding friends,
Onward he press'd, and kept him still in sight;
Then whirl'd aloft his sword with all his might:
Th' unerring steel descended while he spoke,
Pierc'd his wide mouth, and thro' his weazon broke.
Dying, he slew; and stagg'ring on the plain,
With swimming eyes he sought his lover slain;
Then quiet on his bleeding bosom fell,
Content, in death, to be reveng'd so well.
  O happy friends! for, if my verse can give

Immortal life, your fame shall ever live,
Fix'd as the Capitol's foundation lies,
And spread, where'er the Roman eagle flies!

Now Mandelbaum's:

  He spoke,
then, straining all his body, hurled his steel.
Across the shadows of the night it flies,
then strikes the facing back of Sulmo; there
it snaps and, splintered, passes through his midriff.
As Sulmo tumbles over in chill death,
he vomits out a warm stream from his chest;
his long-drawn gasps heave hard against his ribs.
The Latins look around, at every angle.
While they still tremble, Nisus, even fiercer,
now poises a new shaft at his eartip.
The hissing spear drives straight through both the temples
of Tagus; warm, it stuck in his pierced brain.
Though Volcens rages, crazed, he cannot see
whoever was the sender of that shaft
or where he can attack in frenzy. 'Yet
until we find him, you shall pay,' he cried,
'the penalties of both with your warm blood.'
He rushed with drawn sword at Euryalus.
Then, mad with terror, Nisus cries aloud —
he could not hide in darkness anymore
or stand so great a grief: 'I did it — I:
your steel, Rutulians, is meant for me;
the crime is mine; he has not dared anything,
nor could he; heaven be my witness and
the knowing stars: he only loved too well
his luckless friend.' So was he pleading when
the sword, thrust home with force, pierced through
  the ribs
and broke the white breast of Euryalus.
He tumbles into death, the blood flows down
his handsome limbs; his neck, collapsing, leans
against his shoulder: even as a purple
flower, severed by the plow, falls slack in death;
or poppies as, with weary necks, they bow
their heads when weighted down by sudden rain.
But Nisus rushes on among them all;
he is seeking only Volcens, only Volcens
can be the man he wants. The enemy
crowd him; on every side, their ranks would drive

him back, but Nisus presses on unchecked,
whirling his lightning sword until he plunged
it full into the Latin's howling mouth
and, dying, took away his foeman's life.
Then pierced, he cast himself upon his lifeless
friend; there, at last, he found his rest in death.
    Fortunate pair! If there be any power
within my poetry, no day shall ever
erase you from the memory of time;
not while Aeneas' children live beside
the Capitol's unchanging rock nor while
a Roman father still holds sovereignty.

The reader without Latin will be reassured to find that both translators convey the speed, thrust and directness of this passage. Both, moreover, render the flower-simile satisfactorily: Dryden's version is better, partly because he keeps Virgil's three-line structure, and partly because that unexpected adjective 'white' (not in the Latin) picks up and reinforces the white breast (*candida pectora*, 432) of the dying youth and increases the pathos of the simile in a way which seems wholly legitimate. Dryden is also very effective in his rendering of v.430, which he extends into a couplet without seeming to 'pad out' the sense: the extension (again) underlines the pathos of the Latin. Dryden omits the shadows of the night (411) and in general Mandelbaum tries to follow the Latin closely, even attempting an alliterative pattern in the opening lines (straining, steel, strikes, snaps, splintered). Of both versions it may be said (and this is also broadly true of others, notably Fitzgerald's) that far more of the original survives than is lost.

It is as a literary artist that Virgil has survived through twenty centuries. In a recent survey of the poet, Fred Robertson observed that 'if Latin authors ever do fade into oblivion, Virgil will be the last to go', and computed that since 1950 seven translations of the *Aeneid* into English have been published, a spate of versions probably unequalled since the sixteenth century, when the poem was first rendered into English. For most of the life of the poem Latin has been accessible to educated people, but this can now no longer be assumed, so that the modern translator has a much greater responsibility than, say, Dryden had. What, we may ask, remains of a classic poet when his subject matter has become remote and the language he wrote in is dead? How has Virgil survived such formidable obstacles and still remained a central (in Eliot's view, *the* central) figure in European letters? Has he in fact survived them, or are we dealing with a text which survives primarily in what others have felt and said about it?

It has been said that with Virgil 'European poetry grew up': a new sensibility entered the literary scene – sophisticated, elegant, musical, and above all personal. The 'voice' of the author entered unmistakeably into his text. With Virgil we can say, as of certain great poets of the Christian era – Dante, Donne, Wordsworth – that there is something about their literary personae which, though perhaps hard to define, is easy to recognise: something more than, and other than, their actual discourse, permeating that discourse and transcending it. It is the fashion today in some circles to proclaim 'the death of the author' and the emergence of a new reader-centred text; but literary personality cannot so easily be despatched. The reader of the *Aeneid* will become aware more and more, especially in the poem's closing books, of the empathising voice of the 'implied author'. This figure is not to be identified with the narrator who organises the sequence of events, nor with the self-conscious composer of epic (*dicam . . horrida bella*, *arma virumque cano*, etc.), nor with the speculative philosopher of book VI, the journey to the land of the dead ('may I be allowed to reveal things hidden in darkness'); but rather as the omnipresent figure of the creative artist continually involved in every possible nuance of his own text, continually evolving new modes of insight into the human condition; the poet of the flower-similes in book IX and book XI, which T. E. Page thought 'perhaps the most perfect simile in the poem'; the poet who could transform a traditional *topos* into a sentiment in which the reader may find his own feelings refracted:

> Aurora interea miseris mortalibus almam
> extulerat lucem referens opera atque labores
>
> (XI.182–3)
>
> Dawn meanwhile to miserable mortals put forth her kindly
> Light, bringing back work and toil –

the poet who could write of war and the pity of war:

> di Iovis in tectis iram miserantur inanem
> amborum et tantos mortalibus esse labores.
>
> (X.758–9)
>
> The gods in Jupiter's house pity the pointless wrath
> Of either side and all that human effort.

The labours of Virgil's heroes may be remote from us, but the intensity of the poet's empathy and the eloquence of his discourse allow the reader to find in the *Aeneid* the sufferings of all humanity, or, in W. R. Johnson's fine phrase, 'our utter vulnerability and desolation', as well as the moral strength to endure. The word 'endure' *(durate)* occurs in Aeneas' first speech to his shipwrecked fellow-exiles in book I; that speech also contains the celebrated words:

> forsan et haec olim meminisse iuvabit
> maybe one day we shall remember even these sufferings
> with pleasure.

The *Aeneid* survives, and survives greatly, because it is one of the most authentic records we have of human suffering and resilient hope.

14 Narrative technique

It is not easy to grasp the *Aeneid* – or perhaps any long work – 'as a whole'. Critics inevitably select for scrutiny isolated passages which are in some way said to be 'representative' of the whole. But this process cannot help the reader towards a sense of the structure and movement of the entire narrative. Such features as the juxtaposition and relationship of speeches, narrative and descriptive passages, breaks and transitions between 'movements', changes of tempo, location and perspective, cannot be illustrated as easily as similes, alliteration, or expressive sentiments, for they have to be experienced and realised by the reader as he progresses through the poem. Moreover, the reader's sense of these larger features (transitions, changes of location and perspective, etc.) will not be stable or constant in the sense in which it is easy to recognise the same alliterative pattern at every reading. Perhaps the most significant level of reader-response to a long work of fiction, the level at which the mind lingers, is not a verbal level at all but an ideational one, and what we are finally responding to is to events imaginatively recreated, not to word-meanings. At this level questions of translation, which are purely verbal, may cease to be relevant as the reader perceives, or attempts to perceive, a possible answer (and such answers are themselves variables, for our own perceptions change with every reading) to the question of what a long work of fiction is 'about', what it presents. And with any work of fiction of the smallest sophistication, the presentational processes themselves become part of our sense of what is being presented. This is especially true of Virgil's *Aeneid*, in which we are always aware of the modes of presentation, the 'style', as being in a sense what determines the presented narrative, the voice of the 'implied author' directing and manipulating the reader; but in any long literary narrative of proven merit (including Homer's epics, which used to be thought 'naive') our sense of the work 'as a whole' must include our sense of how the narrative is presented.

Some attempt, therefore, must now be made to discuss Virgil's narrative technique, and in particular his mastery of the art of narrative transitions. Let us take a section of book IV (lines 129–278). The action of this passage is swift and dramatic, the set-pieces cosmic in their grandeur. We start with the celebrated 'royal hunt and storm', when Aeneas and Dido ride forth in the bright morning, splendidly attired. The scene is one of colour, movement and excitement. The young hero Ascanius, Aeneas' son, hopes for a boar or for a lion to come down from the mountain. But the reader has just finished a passage in which the two goddesses plot to engineer a 'marriage' between Dido and Aeneas: this is to take place in a cave where the two will shelter from a storm. The storm itself, like the one which begins the poem, is the work of Juno, whose plot this is: Venus agrees to the scheme, for she knows that Aeneas must reach Italy as promised by Jupiter, and that the scheme can thus only work against Dido. It is a cruel trick to play on the unsuspecting queen, and it helps the author to manipulate the reader's sympathy for her, an essential feature of any reading of book IV.

Consequently, when the storm duly breaks, the reader is expecting it, but the characters are not, so there is a balance of anticipation and narrative surprise. The lines which describe how Dido and Aeneas enter the cave pick up Juno's words in her plotting with Venus. Juno had promised:

> speluncam Dido dux et Troianus eandem
> devenient.
> To the same cave Dido and the Trojan chief
> Shall come.

And the narrative makes her promise good − only a change of tense is needed:

> speluncam Dido dux et Troianus eandem
> deveniunt. prima et Tellus et pronuba Juno
> dant signum; fulsere ignes et conscius aether
> conubiis.
> To the same cave Dido and the Trojan chief
> Come. And primal earth and bride-attending Juno
> Give the signal. Lightning flashed, the sky itself
> Witnessed the union.

The heavy, menacing spondees help the reader to feel a sense of impending disaster. After this brilliant and highly charged piece of description come four lines of authorial moral discourse:

> This day was the start of death and woe, the start
> And cause; careless of what men saw or said
> Dido no longer kept her love a secret;
> She hid her guilt under the cloak of marriage.

Dido's 'guilt' (*culpa*) is an allusion both to her vow to be faithful to her dead husband, and also to her self-deceiving and excessive passion for Aeneas, who has no such desire for marriage in his heart. The narrative is now rapidly resumed with the description of Rumour, personified as a monster out of science-fiction, getting bigger and stronger as it moves faster, beginning as a mere wisp of anxiety, feeding on itself till its head touches the sky while its feet remain on the ground, feathered with eyes, tongues, mouths and ears. It flies in the twilight and broods by day on rooftops like the ill-omened bird which will appear as a portent to Dido before she dies, a little further on in book IV. It is a highly pictorial piece of writing, into which the author inserts an epigrammatic and generalising summary of Rumour's function:

> tam ficti pravique tenax quam nuntia veri.
> Messenger alike of wicked lies and truth.

The narrative is now swiftly resumed. Rumour appears to Dido's rejected suitor, Iarbas, who turns to Jupiter, not in prayer but in angry reproach: how dare Jupiter proclaim omnipotence yet allow his servant's feudal lordship to be flouted by Aeneas, whom he calls 'that Paris', a contemptuous allusion to the Homeric hero who ran off with another man's woman. The theme parallels that in the second half of the poem, when Turnus accuses Aeneas of 'taking' Lavinia from him. Both Iarbas and Turnus regard women as chattels.

After a paragraph of narrative directed upon Iarbas, the camera of narrative tracks to Olympus: the transition is made from Iarbas in the nominative to Iarbas in the accusative:

> Him thus praying . . . the Omnipotent heard.
> And turned his eyes on Carthage walls and on
> Two lovers oblivious of their better name.

Jupiter now summons his messenger Mercury and tells him to go to Aeneas with orders to sail at once: has he forgotten his Roman mission? If he does not care about himself, how can he forget his duty to his son?

Again there is a change of subject, this time from Jupiter to Mercury, whose flight to earth offers a parallel to the flight of Rumour; the good messenger contrasted to the bad one: Rumour was a *nuntia*, and Jupiter entrusts to Mercury *nostri nuntius*, our message. The flight of Mercury is one of the great set-pieces of the *Aeneid*. He passes Atlas, who carries the universe on his shoulders, and whom Virgil depicts symbolically as both a giant and a landscape, his head a forest of pines, snow on his shoulders, ice in his beard. It is an extraordinary piece of word-painting, extravagantly baroque, unsurpassed by Milton's description of Satan's flight to earth in *Paradise Lost* II, yet it does not hinder the larger movement of the narrative, for Mercury lands like a bird and sees 'Aeneas founding a citadel', so that we have moved from the seeing Mercury to the seen hero: such spectacular sweeps and scene-changes are almost cinematic in their visual power and control. We have come in 150 lines of verse a long way from a man and a woman sheltering in a cave; yet to Aeneas we now return. Nothing has 'happened' to him since the 'marriage', yet how much has happened in the narrative.

Let us now attempt to consider an even larger piece of narrative discourse, the account of the fall of Troy, which occupies the whole of book II, and which describes one of the most celebrated events in the entire tradition of heroic epic. It so happens that no complete narrative survives written from the Greek point of view: the two primary epics which covered the end of the Trojan war, the *Little Iliad* and the *Sack of Troy* (composed after Homer's epics, probably in the seventh century BC), do not survive; it is not even certain that Virgil had access to complete texts of these works, though he would have known their contents from various summaries and digests of which we ourselves know enough to identify certain episodes in Virgil's account as belonging to the primary epic tradition.

The most obvious, yet also the most striking feature of Virgil's narrative of the fall of Troy is that it is told in the first person by the Trojan survivor Aeneas to Dido; it is a story of defeat, not triumph, told by a lonely storm-battered exile, who has lost his wife, his father and his country. No wonder he is tempted to settle down in the half-built city of Carthage as Dido's co-ruler rather than face again the unknown seas; no wonder, too, that Dido, listening to his tale, kept the talk going through the night 'and drank in long draughts of love' (*longumque bibebat amorem*), so that the reader is reminded of Othello and Desdemona:

> She loved me for the dangers I had passed
> And I loved her, that she did pity them.

The role of Aeneas had to be presented with the greatest tact and skill. He must want to stay on in Troy and fight to the death, yet fate calls him away. He must not seem to have deserted the stricken town, but to have responded to the call of a higher duty: to save Troy's *sacra* (household gods) and pursue his destiny in Italy. How prophetically Dido ought to have understood, and in retrospect interpreted, the events of book II, and how brilliantly Virgil, the authorial voice behind the first-person narrator, presents book II as a structural paradigm of book IV. Early in book II, at the moment when Laocoon thrusts his spear into the wooden horse which has been left behind by the Greeks, who have apparently abandoned the siege, Aeneas says to Dido: 'If fate had not been against us, if our minds had not been deluded, he had surely made us handsel with blood that Greek hiding place, and then, ah, Troy would still be standing, Priam's citadel, you would be there still.'

Dido is to hear that heartfelt sentiment from Aeneas' lips once more, before he leaves her; he says in book IV 'If fate had let me do it my way, I'd have rebuilt Troy, and Priam's citadel would still be there.' At the close of book II Aeneas tells Dido how the shade of his wife Creusa foretold his long journey into exile and eventually to Italy; she commends Aeneas to the future, and to another wife, with her blessing. But that other wife is not fated to be Dido, and from Dido at the end of book IV Aeneas will part without turning back (as he did in his vain search for Creusa in the burning ruins of Troy), and will receive from her not the blessing of history but its dying curse.

Throughout Aeneas' narrative of the fall of Troy a double hindsight operates – the hero's and the author's. Both must try to explain what in retrospect must appear to have been one of the most disastrous failures of judgment ever recorded.

The Trojans' decision that it was right to admit the fatal wooden horse into their city must appear to be the result not of stupidity but of wishful thinking and excessive *pietas*. The wishful thinking is first given expression when Aeneas describes to Dido the incredulous joy with which, for the first time in a decade, the Trojans wandered freely along the beach-head, the Greeks having sailed away, apparently for good; and the sense of amazement with which they gazed upon the huge and mysterious structure which had materialised inexplicably outside their walls. Only one man, the priest Laocoon, possessed, like Cassandra, of ignored insights, sees the truth, but his prophetic words — 'either the Achaeans are hidden within this structure, or it is a siege engine' — words which, if heeded, might have saved Troy, are dismissed.

At this point a new character enters, Sinon, a Greek spy posing as a deserter. Aeneas reports in full his long speech, so that the narrative structure is now Virgil — Aeneas — Sinon: it is as if Aeneas were acting out the role of Sinon for Dido. Sinon's speech is specious but false, and contains some of the most brilliant rhetoric in the poem. He accuses Ulysses of trying to have him put to death, an accusation in itself enough to win him sympathy from his bewildered hearers, for to the Trojans (and the Romans) Homer's clever Odysseus had become debased into the wily and deceitful Ulysses, the man who stole the Palladium, a Trojan talisman sacred to Pallas (Minerva). The horse is said by Sinon to be an offering of atonement by the Greeks to the goddess, which, if the Trojans convey it safely into their town, will ensure that the Greeks are doomed. But it is too big to drag through the gate, so the Trojans actually breach their own walls to get it in, an irony indeed — for later Aeneas tells how he saw, in a vision, the gods themselves dismantling the walls of the doomed city.

Both Sinon's trustworthiness and Laocoon's error seem confirmed when a terrible portent occurs: two snakes slide in from the sea and devour the priest. Events now move rapidly. The Trojans spend the night in feasting and rejoicing, but to Aeneas there appears, dreadfully mutilated, the ghost of Hector, who warns him there is no hope for Troy: 'if any hand might have saved her, mine would have . . . but now you must become the guardian of her *sacra* [the holy *penates*, the household gods of the state religion] and convey them to safety.' This must now be Aeneas' role, no longer just *dux* but *penatiger*, not only soldier but also priest. One priest has died, horribly, another, Panthus, will soon follow; Priam will be slain at his own altar by Achilles' son.

Aeneas thus has an early sanction to escape, but as an epic hero he must fight on, exhibit military prowess as well as *pietas*, and Virgil's problem for the rest of book II (and there is evidence that he had not entirely solved it) was how protractedly, and how plausibly, to keep Aeneas in Troy when his higher duty and mission sanction departure. The most problematic episode in book II concerns Helen, who, Aeneas tells Dido, was discovered cowering in fear as the Greeks swarm in, whereas, in book VI, in the underworld, another mutilated hero, Deiphobus, who had succeeded Paris in Helen's bed, claims that it was Helen who gave the signal to the Greek fleet to return. A not inappropriate ambiguity thus continues to surround the enigmatic figure of Helen even to the end: which side was she finally on? In the *Odyssey* Homer shows her safely home and reconciled to Menelaus, and some critics believe that the episode in *Aeneid* II should be removed and that the account in book VI by Deiphobus is the poet's decisive version of how Helen went over to the Greeks at the end.

The last half of Aeneas' narrative in book II is one of the most powerful and devastating accounts of a holocaust ever penned. Throughout, the words of Panthus ring through our ears:

> venit summa dies et ineluctabile tempus
> Dardaniae. fuimus Troes, fuit Ilium et ingens
> gloria Teucrorum; ferus omnia Iuppiter Argos
> transtulit; incensa Danai dominantur in urbe.
> The last day has come and the inescapable hour
> For Troy. We *were* Trojans, Ilium *was* a town;
> The great glory of our nation is over; angry Jupiter
> To Greece has transferred everything,
> And the Greeks have taken over in the blazing town.

In the chaos of smoke and darkness and the lurid glare of
flames Troy crashes down in ruins, says Aeneas – and here
the implied author's voice is heard in a powerful simile – like
an old tree felled on a mountain. Venus appears to Aeneas in
a vision and shows him the gods dismantling the city walls –
the very Olympians have abandoned the city once renowned
for piety, Homer's holy Ilium. The goddess repeats Hector's
advice – get out now – and promises her son that she will
always be with him as his guide. The aged Anchises at first
declines to leave, fearing he will be a burden, but Aeneas carries him on his back, leading his small son by the hand,
followed by a small band of survivors and bearing the sacred
penates. The last 100 lines of book II are among the most
moving in the poem. Aeneas recalls how every sound terrified
him; the Greeks prowled through the shadows; yet the
escapers were almost in sight of the city gates and safety when
Aeneas realised his wife was missing. Leaving his party he
returns in search of her, like Orpheus seeking Eurydice in the
underworld at the end of the *Georgics*. He retraces his steps
to his own house:

> horror ubique animo, simul ipsa silentia terrent,
> inde domum, si forte pedem, si forte tulisset,
> me refero;
> Horror grips my senses, the very silences terrify,
> But I go back home, in case, just in case, she
> might have made her way there.

That repeated *si forte* must have been spoken by Aeneas to
Dido with a choke in the voice, as also no doubt by the poet
himself, for he was famous for his powers as an actor, when
he read the passage to Augustus. Emotion in poetry can
hardly go further than this.

It is now that the shade of Creusa appears to Aeneas
and encourages him to continue his journey to the river
Tiber:

> illic res laetae regnumque et regia coniunx
> parta tibi;
> There a happy state, a kingdom, and a royal bride
> Await you.

And so the narrative of that terrible and unforgettable night ends as the morning star, the star of Venus, rises over mount Ida, symbolising Venus' promise. Aeneas' narrative of his wanderings continues through book III, but we leave it at the beginning of that book, when he and his fellow-exiles embark:

> cum sociis natoque penatibus et magnis dis.

That phrase *penatibus et magnis dis*, with the great gods and the household *sacra*, the symbols of a religious continuity which war cannot destroy, must surely remind the twentieth century forcibly of the survival of Judaism despite secular destruction. The phrase will occur in the *Aeneid* again, at the end of book VIII, in the account of the sea-battle of Actium, associated not with a defeated refugee but with the victorious Augustus.

15 The World of the dead

The first half of the *Aeneid*, the journey of Aeneas from Troy to Italy, is marked by three great climaxes, placed in the three even-numbered books: the fall of Troy (II), the tragedy of Dido (IV), and the arrival in Italy and descent into the underworld (VI). Book VI with its reflections on the destinies of the human soul and the spiritual structure of the universe, is a central mediating text between pagan and Christian ideas of the after-life; its insights prompted Dante to choose Virgil as his guide through hell and purgatory, and led to his medieval reputation as a magus.

Book VI is also the pivot and turning-point of the whole poem. It has been seen as the hero's 'rite of passage'; from spiritual alienation and near despair through the loss of his wife, his homeland and, most overwhelmingly, his father (whose death occurs in book III), he is 'born again' in the Elysian fields where his father's ghost instructs him in his mission as the first founder of Rome. He returns to the upper world to begin that mission and assume the burden of destiny.

The book begins with the arrival, at last, in Italy, the

'promised land' of so many prophesies throughout the first five books. The Trojans make landfall not at the mouth of the Tiber — they arrive there at the opening of book VII — but further south, on the gulf of Naples at Cumae, a few miles west of Pozzuoli (the ancient Puteoli). Cumae (now Cuma) was reputedly the oldest Greek settlement in Italy, the site of a famous oracle of Apollo and of the cave where dwelt the prophetess of Apollo, the Sibyl, whom Aeneas has been ordered to consult and who will guide him through the under-world. Nearby is Lake Avernus, where Virgil locates the actual descent into Hades. For the purpose of his narrative Virgil regards the two sites as contiguous, and conflates the oracle at Cumae with a supposed cult of the dead at Avernus: he often uses the name Avernus as synonymous with Hades itself, as in the famous phrase used by the Sibyl, 'facilis descensus Averno': 'it is easy to descend into hell'.

Cumae is now a deserted ruin, little frequented by tourists. Here a strange and impressive man-made cave was discovered in 1932: it is generally accepted that Virgil had seen this and used it as the basis of his own highly poetic description of the Sibyl's cave. Along the avenue leading to it have been placed marble tablets inscribed with the awe-inspiring verses in which the poet narrates the journey to the underworld.

> Ibant obscuri sola sub nocte per umbram,
> perque Domos ditis vacuas et inania regna.
> Obscure they went through dreary shades that led
> Along the waste dominions of the dead. (Dryden)

Above the cave, reached by a lonely and winding path, is the acropolis of the former city, with the ruins of a great temple later converted into a Christian basilica. From this summit, a steep, wooded and almost inaccessible slope drops down towards the sea. Here, then, Aeneas landed.

Lake Avernus is not now directly accessible from Cumae. Greek tradition had long associated it with Homer's land of the Cimmerians, shrouded in perpetual darkness, where Odysseus was sent to consult the ghost of the prophet Teiresias. Circe's home had also been localised in Italy, at

Monte Circeio between Cumae and Rome: Aeneas sails past
it at the beginning of book VII on his way to the Tiber. There
is no evidence that any underworld cult or entrance actually
existed at Lake Avernus in Virgil's time, but it is easy to see
how a poetic construct could have been fashioned out of its
traditional links with Homer's Odysseus and its proximity to
the prophetic cave of the Sibyl at Cumae.

Book VI is about ghosts and supernatural experiences,
themes already touched on earlier in the poem but almost
entirely absent from books VII–XII. Aeneas' encounter in
book VI with the mutilated ghost of Deiphobus, slain at
Troy, recalls his dream of the mutilated ghost of Hector in
book II. And two earlier appearances of his father's ghost are
decisive in determining Aeneas' actions in the first half of the
poem. In book IV, Anchises' ghost calls him away from
Carthage, as he himself tells Dido:

> me patris Anchisae . . .
> admonet in somnis et turbida terret imago
>
> (IV.351–3)
>
> Nightly in my dreams my father's perturbed spirit
> Admonishes me.

Shakespeare's phrase 'perturbed spirit' is an appropriate
translation, for the appearance of Hamlet's ghost to chide
his son for delaying his mission exactly parallels these
appearances of Anchises' ghost to Aeneas in Carthage.

And in book V Anchises' ghost instructs him to visit the
Sibyl as soon as he arrives in Italy, so that she can lead him
to the underworld where father and son will meet again, and
for the last time:

> Ditis tamen ante
> infernas accede domos et Averna per alta
> congressus pete, nate, meos. non me impia namque
> Tartara habent, tristes umbrae, sed amoena piorum
> concilia Elysiumque colo. huc casta Sibylla
> nigrarum multo pecudum te sanguine ducet.
>
> (V.731–6)

First make your way
To the halls of Dis in the deep underworld
And meet with me, not in Tartarus the wicked
Among the gloomy shades, but in Elysium
In the lovely gatherings of the blessed.
After due sacrifice of black cattle
The holy Sibyl shall lead you there.

Aeneas' meeting with Anchises in the Elysian fields is one of
the great emotional climaxes of the poem. His father sees him
approach, and with tears of joy and outstretched hands
speaks first:

venisti tandem, tuaque expectata parenti
vicit iter durum pietas? datur ora tueri,
nate, tua et notas audire et reddere voces?
sic equidem ducebam animo rebarque futurum
tempora dinumerans, nec me mea cura fefellit.
quas ego te terras et quanta per aequora vectum
accipio! quantis iactatum, nate, periclis!
quam metui ne quid Libyae tibi regna nocerent!
(VI.687–694)

Have you come at last then? and has the filial love
Your father looked for brought you safely over the hard
    way?
Can I really see you, hear you, speak to you, my
    son?
this is what I kept thinking would happen,
Counting the time, nor were my hopes deceived.
After what journeys over land and sea do you
    come
And I receive you now, after what perils,
And how I worried lest you came to harm in
    Libya.

Up to this point, the Sibyl has been Aeneas' guide to the
mysteries of the lower world, but now Anchises takes over,
and his role as teacher is emphasised: *te tua fata docebo*, 'I
shall instruct you in your destiny'. This instruction reaches its
climax in the great pageant of the future (as yet unborn)
heroes of Rome: Romulus, Augustus, the early kings, the
great republicans. This grand Roman conclusion to book VI

can easily be taken out of its mysterious context and compared with other passages in the poem in which we see the greatness of Rome: Jupiter's first prophecy to Venus in book I, the Shield given to Aeneas by Venus in book VIII on which Vulcan has depicted events in Roman history from the story of Romulus to the triumph of Augustus at Actium. But more must be said in the present chapter about the rest of book VI, which represents the most impressive version we have of the traditional epic *topos* of the hero's visit to the underworld.

Virgil's epic model is Odysseus' journey to the land of ghosts in *Odyssey* 11. Odysseus was not the first Greek hero to undertake this perilous journey: the remote and mysterious figure of Orpheus and the great pre-Trojan heroes Theseus and Heracles had also gone to the world of the dead; so had the Sumerian epic hero Gilgamesh. A belief in some form of personal survival after death was widespread among early civilisations, Egyptian, near eastern and mediterranean, and journeys by the living to consort and consult with the dead are concerned with man's earliest attempts to conceptualise the demarcation between mortality and immortality. The latter was regarded as the distinguishing privilege of the gods, but a few favoured heroes succeeded in crossing this divide.

Odysseus was sent to the land of the dead by the enchantress Circe (see the end of *Odyssey* 10) to consult the ghost of the blind seer Teiresias about his own future. Teiresias alone among the dead possesses this prophetic power, the other ghosts whom the hero meets being only able to recall the past. Homer locates the land of ghosts not underground but on a remote shore at the edge of the world, in the country of the Cimmerians, a people who never see the sun. His topography, however, is very vague; the rivers of Hades are named, and there is a reference to the fields of asphodel, but although Homer is clearly drawing on traditional mythology, his primary interest is not in creating atmosphere or in providing a coherent map of hell, but in the various encounters with dead souls whom the hero knew in life — his mother, Agamemnon, Achilles. At the end of book 11 a few examples are mentioned of famous sinners punished for acts of impiety (Tantalus, Sisyphus), but these episodes seem perfunctory and appear to belong to a different convention in which the hero walks about among the dead. The main part of Odysseus' *nekuia* is not a descent among the dead but an evocation of them (cf. Shakespeare's Glendower in *Henry IV part 1*, 'I can call spirits from the vasty deep'). Odysseus digs a ditch, sacrifices animals, and when the blood runs into the ditch the souls flock to him. Homeric ghosts are weak and feeble ('the strengthless heads of the dead' is Homer's phrase) and need to drink blood (cf. vampires) before they can speak. Nor does Homer, despite the presence of the famous sinners of early mythology, envisage any general system of rewards and punishments for mortals in accordance with how they have lived their lives: thus the souls of the frivolous suitors, slain by Odysseus, simply join the great heroes of Troy. However, in *Odyssey* 4 the Old Man of the Sea prophesies to Menelaus that he will escape death and go to the Elysian fields 'where life is made easiest for mortals, for there is no snow there, nor much winter, nor rain, but always breezes from the west to refresh mortals'. This description of Paradise closely resembles the description in *Odyssey* 6 of the home of the gods on Olympus: it appears that Homer envisaged the survival of a chosen few in conditions similar to those said to have been enjoyed by the first race of men (the so-called 'golden age'). This myth is expounded by Homer's younger contemporary Hesiod in his *Works and Days*. Not until Pindar (early 5th century BC) do we find the concept of such a life being available to all the just, as a reward after death and judgement in Hades.

Virgil's Elysian fields are apparently reached through the underworld: Aeneas and the Sibyl arrive at a point in their journey where the way divides, the road on the left leading to Tartarus, that on the right to Elysium. They do not visit Tartarus, which is closed to the righteous, but the Sibyl explains that there Rhadamanthus, judge of the dead, reproves the souls of sinners, forcing them to confess crimes committed on earth for which they had put off expiation until too late. Hero and guide then proceed to the Elysian fields: 'Virgil's narrative passes into a dwelling of

light, in an apocalyptic vision of bliss and rewarded virtue'
(Austin):

> devenere locos laetos et amoena virecta
> fortunatorum nemorum sedesque beatas.
> largior hic campos aether et lumine vestit
> purpureo, solemque suum, sua sidera norint.
> They came to the happy land and the pleasant green
> Of the fortunate fields, the seats of the blessed.
> Here an ampler air clothes the meadows in dazzling light
> With its own sun, its own stars.   (VI, 638–641)

These beautiful lines, taken together with a striking phrase
used later in book VI, 'the wide fields of the air', may suggest
that we have transcended the localised tradition of the isles of
blessed and have attained a kind of Platonic, even near-
Christian paradise, lit by its own supernatural light. But
Anchises now explains to Aeneas that this is not the final
home of the soul, but a resting-place, a kind of pastoral tran-
sit camp. The doctrine of metempsychosis or reincarnation
which Anchises will now expound to Aeneas was not part of
any officially held theology, but was associated with
Pythagoras and the Orphic mystery religions; it finds its first
expression in Greek literature in Pindar and influenced
Plato's *Phaedrus*. Much of the imagery in Anchises' speech
comes from this tradition.

It is important to remember the dramatic and narrative
context of Anchises' speech. A metaphysical explanation is
required to account for the pageant of future heroes of Rome.
Aeneas sees a crowd of souls waiting by a river: Anchises explains that they are awaiting the summons to new bodies and
must drink of the waters of Lethe to secure forgetfulness of
their past lives. Aeneas, his own sufferings far from forgotten, asks in amazement:

> Why should sublime souls want to return to sluggish
> bodies? What is this terrible longing for life?

And it is in answer to this sad question that Anchises makes
his great speech, unfolding the mysteries of the soul's
progress from death through purgatory to rebirth, and

eventually to reunion with that divine spark whence it came.

Anchises might say with St Paul, 'behold I show you a mystery', and indeed *Aeneid* VI is a narrative of initiation. Aeneas is enabled to journey into the world of the dead because he becomes an initiate. Just before the descent begins, the Sibyl utters the Orphic formula *procul, o procul este, profani*: 'stand apart, ye profane', (that is, those who are not fit for the mysteries); Aeneas is admitted through his own virtue and because he has secured the Golden Bough, the mysterious talisman which will guarantee him safe passage, a ritual offering to appease Persephone and a protection against corruption. The poet himself offers a solemn prayer and invocation to the chthonic (underworld) deities: 'may it be lawful to me to reveal things hidden in darkness'. The solemnity of the narrative, and the sense of awe and strangeness which Virgil's poetry generates, lend power and authenticity to a world-view which is neither wholly consistent nor wholly coherent, but which is full of spiritual insights and memorable images.

Anchises' speech is written in the unmistakable didactic style of Virgil's great predecessor Lucretius, who in his poem *On the Nature of Things* had rejected immortality and set forth a materialistic philosophy. It is as if Virgil were applauding the style of this famous poem while repudiating its matter. The opening of the speech is full of Lucterian echoes:

> Principio caelum ac terras camposque liquentis
> lucentemque globum lunae Titaniaque astra . . .
> To begin with, the heavens, the earth, the sea, the
> cosmos, are infused and activated by a creative mind.
> This spiritual energy, pure elemental fire, is in
> all living things; all have a heavenly origin.
> Particles of this divine nature cling to us
> throughout life, even though the soul is clogged by
> the body, in which it is shut as in a dark prison.
> After death, some ingrained evil remains, which must
> be purged by punishment through wind, water, and fire.
> Each of us must undergo our own treatment as spirits,

until at last we are sent to Elysium, where in the fulness of
time, when the last stain of sin is gone, a few of us become
ethereal fire. All the rest, after a cycle of a thousand years, are
called by the god to Lethe to prepare for rebirth.

(VI, 734–751)

This strange and haunting synthesis of religion, mysticism,
cosmology and mythology is composed of ideas and images
put together from various sources — thus Stoicism contributed the idea of the 'world-soul' or *anima mundi*, the
originating ethereal fire of creation; Platonism contributed
the idea of the thousand-year cycle of rebirth; the image of
the body as the prison of the soul is from Orphic mysticism;
while bogey-figures like Charon the ferryman and Cerberus
the three-headed dog, along with various giants, monsters
and archetypal sinners, are recurrent features of Greek myth,
familiar enough for parody (see Aristophanes' *The Frogs*).
Christianity would drop the concepts of reincarnation and
reunion with the *anima mundi*, but would develop the process
of purgation and turn the Elysian fields into the eternal home
of the blessed.

But the enigmas of *Aeneid* VI are not quite concluded.
After his cosmological lecture, Anchises identifies for Aeneas
the as yet unborn heroes of the future Roman state. If we ask
how souls still awaiting reincarnation can already present the
adult appearance of characters they have not yet assumed, we
can only answer — by magic. And it is magic that has the last
word. Anchises briefly warns his son that he will soon have
to fight to establish a home in Latium. He does not give
details, for the very good reason that this war will form the
narrative of books IX–XII. The Sibyl then escorts Aeneas out
of Hades by the ivory gate which is the gate of false dreams.
Why not by the gate of horn, the gate of true dreams, for
surely the historical pageant, if not the cosmological speculation, is self-validating? Virgil has taken the figure of the two
gates from Homer, *Odyssey* 19, 560–7, where Penelope says
that deceptive dreams come to us through the ivory gate,
'their message is never accomplished', but those which issue
through the gate of horn come to pass.

In this concluding image Virgil seems to sum up the 'undecidabilities' of book VI. What if the whole episode were a dream, like that dream of the younger Scipio, recorded by Cicero in his *Republic*, in which the elder Scipio appeared to his son and showed him the order of the universe and the rewards which await those who have served the state well? It has been suggested that because Aeneas is not himself a *vera umbra*, a true ghost, he cannot leave by the gate of horn. In the world of shadows it is perhaps he who is 'unreal'. He has seen things the living ought not to see, and his vision of them can never be validated outside that 'other dimension'. Certainly they are never mentioned or referred to again — a strange interlude in the tale of epic heroism now to be resumed.

16 Father-figures

The *Aeneid* is dominated by fathers and father-figures. Jupiter is called 'father of men and gods' and Aeneas himself is called *pater* as often as he is called *pius*: not only is he literally a father, and will inaugurate through his son the line of Roman kings, but in general the term *pater* signifies moral responsibility. Aeneas' relationship with other paternal figures is an important element in the moral structure of the poem. Two such figures appear in books I–VI: Anchises, who disappears from the narrative after the underworld episode, and Priam, king of Troy, whose sacrilegious death at his own altar, where he had sought sanctuary in vain, is recounted by Aeneas to Dido in book II. He says to Dido 'I thought of my own father when I saw the king cruelly wounded and breathing his last, for they were the same age.'

In the second half of the poem Virgil introduces two other elderly princes who may be said to inherit something of the roles of Priam and Anchises, and who are important in the narrative of books VII and VIII: these are transitional books between peace and war, in the course of which Aeneas tries to make peaceful terms with the indigenous inhabitants of

Latium, with only partial success. In book VII Aeneas sends an embassy to negotiate with Latinus, king of Latium. His daughter Lavinia is promised to a local chieftain, Turnus, but an oracle has told him that she must marry a foreign prince who is destined to rule in Latium and make the Latin name world-famous. Latinus recognises Aeneas as the promised son-in-law and offers him a peaceful alliance.

Latinus is an Italian Priam. His citadel is grandly built, yet it is set in pastoral surroundings and is the home of the old religions of Italy, going back to Saturn, who, according to Virgil, settled in Latium after being thrown out of Olympus by his usurping son Jupiter, and there established a kind of 'golden age'. Much is made of the predominantly peaceful nature of the land to which the Trojans have come. Latinus' peace is also, however, the peace of old age and weakness. When Turnus, threatened with the loss of his promised bride, decides to make war on the Trojans independently of the king, Latinus is too weak to resist and relinquishes his authority, retiring into his citadel somewhat as Priam had retreated to his altar when faced by the invading Greeks.

Parallel with Latinus is another father-figure who dominates book VIII. Evander, like Latinus, belongs to the various myths and legends of primitive Italy freely adapted by Virgil for the purposes of his own narrative. He was a Greek from Arcadia supposed to have emigrated to the site of the future Rome before the Trojan war, and to have founded the settlement of Pallanteum on the Palatine hill. He is said to have known Anchises, and there is a sense in which he takes Anchises' place in the second half of the poem as the supporter and guide of Aeneas. Aeneas seeks him out in fulfilment of the Sibyl's prophecy that he would need help from a Greek city; their encounter in book VIII offers significant parallels with the encounter between Aeneas and Anchises in Elysium. Just as Aeneas receives first-hand guidance in the Elysian fields, so now he receives first-hand guidance in the very place where one day the city of Rome will arise.

Both the seventh and eighth books sustain the mood of pastoral peace established in the Elysian fields. Indeed, there is no finer example of narrative transition in the whole poem than that at the beginning of book VII, when Aeneas sails past the home of Circe (see above, pp. 76–7) on his way from Cumae to the Tiber. The weird groans of men transformed by witchcraft into beasts are heard in the night, but gradually give way to a dawn-chorus of familiar birds as the Trojans reach the mouth of the Tiber. In book VIII, Virgil emphasises the pastoral simplicity of Evander's hut-settlement and contrasts it with the splendours of the Augustan metropolis. This contrast between 'then' and 'now' is not exploited in order to denigrate contemporary achievement, but rather to remind the Romans of their simple beginnings – Evander's poor settlement, the pastoral cave in which the wolf suckled the baby Romulus. When Aeneas the mighty epic hero has to stoop to enter Evander's simple hut, he is exhorted to 'dare to despise wealth'. The moral precept corresponds to Anchises' exhortation to his son to stand firm in Latium and to extend his reputation by the exercise of virtue. In the last book of the poem Aeneas himself passes on this advice to *his* son:

> Learn from me, my son, the true exercise of
> Virtue and hard work, but for good luck look elsewhere.

It is not in man's power to control Fortune, but it is in his power to exercise virtue and to labour truly for the right.

Not only does Evander entrust his son Pallas to Aeneas as Latinus had entrusted to him his daughter Lavinia – Pallas' death at the hand of Turnus is central to the Iliadic plot of books IX–XII (see above, pp. 33–4) – but he also acts as Aeneas' guide on a lecture-tour round the site of Rome, welcoming him to Pallanteum much as Anchises had welcomed him to Elysium, teaching him about the past as Anchises had taught him about the future. Thus both Anchises and Evander, speaking with the insight and authority of age and knowledge, serve as mouthpieces for a series of authorial disquisitions on the origin and significance of what Aeneas sees. Evander may perhaps be a *persona* of Virgil, guiding the new *dux* (Augustus) to the city which he is to be instrumental in re-founding, and showing that its origins are even older than the coming of his Trojan ancestor. Various features of the Rome of Virgil's own day are mentioned: this is not anachronism but rather a deliberate 'synchronism', by which the reader sees through his own eyes as well as through those of Aeneas. The reader is of course the implied Augustan reader: when the Capitol is described as 'golden now, but in those days bristling with thickets yet already imbued with religious awe', the implied reader would have thought of the great temple of Jupiter Capitolinus with its roof of gold. By an irony of history, the modern reader will think of a Rome closer to Evander's than to that of Augustus, a Rome whose great imperial monuments are now ruins. Just as Anchises made Aeneas discern, in the souls awaiting rebirth, the lineaments of the Roman heroes they were destined to become, so Evander makes him discern, in the caves, rocks and groves of primitive Pallanteum, the monuments of the future city.

This guided tour is accompanied by a lecture on the legendary origins of Latium. A golden age was established by Saturn when he was thrown out of Olympus by Jupiter, but that civilisation of peaceful and voluntary obedience to law and custom was not sustained by later generations. The old values, Virgil is saying, gave way to war and greed and this deterioration signals the need for a new dispensation in Italy – and by a further synchronism, this new dispensation is both that which Aeneas will bring and that which Augustus will bring. Aeneas' immediate task is to re-establish, at the cost of war if need be, the simple moral traditions which Evander and Latinus have tried to preserve but are too old to defend unaided.

The walk round the site of Rome offers a topographical narrative sequence parallel to the historical sequence of events 'prophetically' presented to Aeneas in the form of pictures carved by Vulcan on the Shield given to the hero by his mother Venus in the scene which ends book VIII. When he looks at these pictures, Aeneas can only wonder – as he wondered during the walk around Pallanteum, as he wondered in Elysium – at events and characters so far beyond his immediate comprehension. Aeneas is said to enjoy the pictures on the Shield without understanding the reality they portray — a reality which lies, for him, far in the future; the modern reader may also find himself enjoying the experience of reading the poem but missing its historical dimension, which for him lies not in the remote future but in the remote past. The *Aeneid* is a text of shifting historical perspectives.

Aeneas' walk with Evander ends on the Palatine, where Evander's house is located. The climax of the events depicted on the Shield of Aeneas is the dedication on the same site of the great temple of Apollo, erected by Augustus after his victory at Actium. Vulcan's representation on the Shield of these and other coming events offers another parallel with Anchises in Elysium. Vulcan is also described as *pater*: he is gifted with insights, *haud vatum ignarus venturique inscius aevi*, 'not unacquainted with the prophets nor ignorant of the age to come', and is thus another persona of the poet himself. In Augustan Rome the old Roman word *vates* was used for 'poet' as well as for 'prophet', ousting the Greek 'poeta'. There is no doubt that through his various venerable mouthpieces Virgil took seriously the artist's vatic responsibility. The role of the father-figure, like that of the poet, is a didactic one. Aeneas the refugee must become Aeneas the initiate, Aeneas the learner, before he is ready to assume the burden of history. This burden he symbolically and finally assumes at the end of book VIII, when he puts on the prophetic shield. He will now 'carry' the Roman universe like his mythical burden-shouldering predecessors, Atlas and Hercules.

17 Juno

Anchises, Evander, and (until his authority is swept aside by Turnus) Latinus all help to forward Aeneas' mission; his most formidable impediment, however, is not male but female, and not mortal but a goddess.

Most of the plot of the *Aeneid* is generated by Juno,

sister and consort of Jupiter. She is Homer's Hera, who in the
Iliad was implacably anti-Trojan, primarily because of the
'judgement of Paris', the celebrated divine beauty contest
between three goddesses, Hera, Athene and Aphrodite
(Venus). Each offered the judge, Paris, a bribe; Aphrodite offered Helen, wife of the Greek hero Menelaus, and won,
which led to the Trojan war.

Virgil refers to Juno's ancient grudge early in the poem, in
concise and memorable phrases:

> manet alta mente repostum
> iudicium Paridis spretaeque iniuria formae.
>
> (I.25–6)
>
> there sticks deep in her heart
> the judgment of Paris and the insult to her spurned beauty.

Not only does Juno have this personal resentment; she is also
mindful of how the Trojans fought against her cherished
Greeks, and she knows that her favourite city, Carthage, is
destined by fate to be one day destroyed by a race of Trojan
blood (the Romans). When the poem opens, Aeneas is close
to the shore of Carthage; if Juno could shipwreck him there
it would be an ironic perversion of destiny. But he lands
safely at Carthage, though there too Juno has an instrument
at hand – Dido. Juno's attempts to thwart or pervert the
Trojans' survival and the providential course of history continue until the very end of the poem.

Both halves of the *Aeneid* begin with a soliloquy by Juno
in which she reflects angrily on her humiliating failure –
despite the fact that she is queen of heaven – to prevent the
Trojans from fulfilling their destiny. When we first meet
Juno in book I she is described as 'aeternum servans sub pec-
tore vulnus', 'nursing in her heart an eternal wound', and that
motif of the psychological 'wound' recurs in connection with
her protégés Dido and Turnus (see above, pp. 44–6). In book
I the goddess sees the Trojans making for Italy, and determines to delay their arrival by arranging with Aeolus, a minor
deity in charge of the winds, to send a storm which prolongs the
Trojans' misery: some ships are sunk, and Aeneas himself is

cast ashore at Carthage. In this soliloquy Juno expresses her hatred of Aeneas in a war-metaphor: *una cum gente tot annos bella gero*, 'I wage war for so many years with a single nation', and in the corresponding soliloquy which opens book VII she begins to make war literally, calling to her aid a more terrible agent than Aeolus: a Fury out of hell, Allecto, is summoned to arouse Turnus to arms. In a memorably epigrammatic line Juno declares *flectere si nequeo superos, Acheronta movebo* — 'if I can't influence the powers above, I'll move those below.' The line is perfectly symmetrical, beginning and ending with a verb, and perhaps was in Milton's mind when he gave Satan his famous words (*Paradise Lost* 1.263) 'better to reign in hell than serve in heaven.'

In a powerful passage the Fury manifests herself to Turnus in a dream — a bad dream in contrast to the good visions of Aeneas: *bella manu letumque gero*, 'I carry war and death in my hands', she says: Turnus wakes sweating with fear, but the insidious subliminal message has got home. Juno has succeeded in transferring her own anger and hatred to Turnus, who now calls for arms: *saevit amor ferri et scelerata insania belli, ira super* (VII.461–2): 'love of the sword rages in him, and wicked war-madness, and wrath as well' (against Aeneas). *Saevit* picks up the adjective *saeva*, fierce, used of Juno earlier in book VII. Thus the war which occupies the last four books of the poem is the enactment of Juno's hatred. If she cannot in the long run alter destiny, the declared will of Jupiter, she can yet exact a terrible price in blood for Lavinia's wedding to Aeneas, as she says in the last words of her great soliloquy:

> sanguine Troiano et Rutulo dotabere, virgo,
> et Bellona manet te pronuba.
> Your dowry, virgin, shall be Trojan and Rutulian blood,
> Bellona, goddess of war, shall be the bride's matron.
>
> (VII. 318–19)

The Rutuli are the tribe headed by Turnus; Bellona was an Italian war-goddess, and a *pronuba* in the Roman marriage-ceremony was the matron who was in charge of the bride. Juno herself was the Roman goddess of marriage so the words have a dreadful irony, especially when we recall that she herself had acted as celestial *pronuba* in the disastrous pseudo-marriage of Dido to Aeneas. It is characteristic of Juno, as it is indeed of the madness of war, to spare neither side; she does not care what it costs as long as she has her way; Dido is sacrificed, and ultimately Turnus too. The whole of this passage is full of the language of hatred, war-fury and the spilling of blood. The coming conflict between indigenous and immigrant peoples who are destined to become one nation is described as *discordia*, civil war, to the Roman of Virgil's day the worst kind of war. Jupiter himself uses the same word when he angrily denounces Juno in book X for stirring up strife against his will. It is clear that if Juno can act against the divine will she can be seen as both embodying and generating that sense of moral bewilderment which accompanies every apparently successful manifestation of evil.

The stirring up of war in Latium, contrary not only to the will of Jupiter but to that of king Latinus, is Juno's masterpiece. It is she herself who at VII. 622, 'opened the iron gates of war': Virgil has adapted a phrase of Ennius in which it is Discordia which opens the gates. It is clear that for Virgil Juno embodies the dreaded spirit of civil strife. Yet once the war has started, her power begins to diminish as events move towards their destined end. In book X she is allowed to rescue Turnus temporarily from the battle, but Jupiter warns her not to base any false hopes on this respite: 'If you think you can change the whole course of the war, you nurse a vain hope.' But this is exactly what Juno does hope. She says to Jupiter: 'What if your words belied your true thoughts, and Turnus was going to be saved. But oh let me be deceived by false hope, and may you change your will — for it is in your power.' (X. 622–32). Juno has a premonition of the end, yet, as people do when they know in their secret heart that something is inevitable yet retain a half-real half-pretended reservation that even now, against all the odds, at the eleventh hour, it may turn out well, so Juno leaves a tiny crack of light; in her heart the door of fate is not yet quite shut against Turnus, there is still time for all-powerful Jupiter to change

his mind. Juno's secret hope against hope is shared by her
protégés Dido and Turnus, both of whom attempt to pervert
the course of destiny but are forced in the end to admit defeat
and pay a terrible price for their self-deception.

Virgil's treatment of Juno shows great psychological insight. Her *idée fixe*, her obsessional hatred of Troy, provides
the motivation of the entire poem. Only at the end of book
XII does she admit defeat and become reconciled to destiny.
This is necessary, for Juno was, after all, a great Roman goddess: Jupiter had prophesied to Venus in book I that Juno
'will have second, and better thoughts, and with me will
cherish the Roman nation.' This happens in book XII. In
return for yielding to destiny and accepting Aeneas' victory,
Juno asks only that the names of Troy and Trojan be wholly
expunged from history, and that the new nation be Italian
and Roman, a request which Jupiter smilingly agrees to, for
it is what was intended all along.

This motif of Juno's reconciliation to Rome is a recurring
one: Horace suggests (*Odes* 3.1) that the goddess later agreed
to the deification of Romulus on the same terms. She is also
said to have abandoned Carthage after its defeat by Rome,
and the Roman republican hero Camillus was said to have
transferred her image to Rome from Veii after the defeat of
that city. Her worship was widespread throughout Italy, and
consequently flourished in many places which became
Rome's enemies, but there was a belief among the ancients
that the gods abandoned doomed cities, as they did Troy: this
tradition is referred to in *Aeneid* II. 326–7, 351–2. Jupiter
himself is there said to have handed over Troy to the Greeks;
in book XII Turnus, at the end of his life, says that the gods
and Jupiter have abandoned him. So we may feel that Juno's
reconciliation with Aeneas is only one of a series of such
changes of side, prompted not by any kind of moral repen-
tance but in response to military and historical necessity.
Nevertheless, Jupiter's final words in the poem, echoing his
words to Venus in book I, promise Juno a secure and
honoured place in the Roman pantheon: the new nation
which will arise from the mingling of Italian and Trojan

blood through Lavinia's marriage to Aeneas 'will surpass all others in *pietas* and no nation will honour you more than they will'. This reconciliation of opposites is the true resolution of the poem.

18 War and heroism

The last four books of the *Aeneid* depict the war in Latium between the Trojans and their allies — who include Arcadians led by Pallas and Etruscans under Tarchon — and the Italians led by Turnus, chief of the tribe of the Rutuli. Turnus' allies include Camilla queen of the Volsci, the exiled Etruscan tyrant Mezentius, and many other aboriginal chiefs who parade before the reader at the end of book VII in the famous 'gathering of the clans' (in Warde Fowler's happy phrase). They are a motley crew, semi-barbarous, semi-mythical, and represent the old Italy whose blood is destined to mingle with the blood of Troy to form a new nation.

The war occupies only a few weeks (in the old Roman chronicles it lasted on and off for years), and this telescoping of the action gives urgency and intensity to the narrative, and contrasts with the diffuse and often digressive presentation by Homer of the events of the *Iliad* — events which themselves occupy only a few weeks but which form part of a ten-year struggle still going on when the poem ends. Virgil ends his poem with a treaty between Latinus and Aeneas to which Turnus is the only remaining obstacle (Mezentius and Camilla having both been killed). Aeneas and Turnus meet in single combat, as had Hector and Achilles, but Homer's duel did not end the war, though it foreshadowed an eventual Greek victory; this time the Trojan will be victorious and the ancient defeat at last expunged.

Virgil's war-narrative does, however, contain may echoes of, and references to, Homer: such features as similes, divine interventions and, above all, the hall-mark of heroic epic, the *aristeia*. Sarpedon's speech to Glaucus in *Iliad* XII well sums up Homer's ideal of the heroic code: heroes are honoured among lesser men, and must repay these honours by fighting; the victorious will win further renown; but there would be no point at all in fighting if we could run away to immortality. It is the ever-present 'spirits of death standing close about in their thousands, no man can escape them', which lends risk and meaning to heroic *aristeia* – that, and the all-important question of reputation. It is notable that Sarpedon in his speech quotes the imaginary words of an ordinary soldier, to the effect that his masters are worthy of kingship and its honours because they know how to fight; and throughout the *Iliad* reputation, often expressed in the comments of others, is of prime importance to a hero.

In the *Aeneid* this view of the epic hero still survives in what after all purports to be a story set in the heroic age of Homer's Troy; but it does not go unchallenged, and the poem is to a large extent an account of how an archaic value-system is superseded. In the character of Turnus, however, Virgil has created an old-style Homeric hero dedicated to personal glory and the protection and enhancement of his own reputation. He too is deeply affected by what people say of him: in the great debate in book XI about whether or not to continue the war or sue for peace Turnus is, of course, all for fighting on, and is particularly stung by a taunt of his opponent Drances, who wants peace, that he should admit that he is already defeated. He recalls this taunt in book XII when he says that he will never surrender and that his right hand will refute Drances' words. Turnus is brave but foolhardy, above all violent and uncontrolled, as was Homer's Achilles after his friend Patroclus was killed; but Achilles showed pity and humanity at the end of the *Iliad* by giving back Hector's body to Priam. Turnus is allowed no such redemptive opportunity; the poem ends with his death and his last words are noble but self-vaunting (see above, p. 46). So too are the last words of the fierce and impious Mezentius, who has seen his son perish at the hand of Aeneas; his famous words to his horse – 'Rhaebus, we've lived a long time, if anything mortal can be said to last long' – are a characteristic expression of the 'implied author's' sense of the pathos and transitoriness of human life. But we are still essentially in the world of Homer's mortality — the only choice is death or glory.

Wholly individualistic also is Camilla, the half-pastoral, half-Amazon warrior-maid whose *aristeia* dominates book XI: she is glamourised by the poet and the cavalry action which she leads is one of the most splendid set-pieces in the poem and a good example of Virgilian updating of Homeric military techniques, for there are no cavalry in the *Iliad*. But she brings about her own downfall by her blind and selfish pursuit of a single Trojan whose gear attracts her.

Camilla's simple pastoral origins are perhaps more important than her rash and imprudent death. In a beautiful biographical digression Virgil recalls, as he did in the peaceful scenes of books VII and VIII, the simple origins of primitive Italy. Camilla was brought up by her father to be hard, to hunt and be self-sufficient, and this Italian toughness is emphasised by the Italian hero Numanus, who unflatteringly contrasts it with Trojan oriental 'softness'.

One of Virgil's chief problems in writing the *Aeneid* was that he did not wish to devalue the sturdy heroism of the aboriginal Italians, while at the same time the Trojans must avenge their defeat at the hands of the Greeks. So he made his Italians brave, but unable to see beyond their own parish and their own lives.

A thirst for individual glory is thus the prime motivation of many of the heroes in the *Aeneid* no less than in the *Iliad*. At the same time, Virgil created in Aeneas a new type of Stoic hero, willing and ready to subordinate his individual will to that of destiny, the commonwealth and the future, reluctant to fight and not really interested in victory. As he says in book XII when he and Latinus strike their peace-treaty, both sides shall be undefeated ('invictae') and shall keep their own laws: neither shall impose conditions on the other. And in book XI, when the Italians request a truce for the burial of the dead, Aeneas again asserts his desire for peace and wishes he could extend to the living the truce he grants for the dead. His language is, in R. D. Williams' phrase, 'curiously modern' in comparison with the language of

Turnus, but it is also deeply Roman, the language of the *pax Augusta*.

But Aeneas, when he must fight, fights as savagely and with as much *furor* as any other hero in the poem; this atavism has been criticised but is central to Virgil's theme, which is that war is madness and that it spares none who engage in it. Aeneas is at his most violent in book X after Pallas has been killed by Turnus: Virgil's model for his conduct here is clearly Achilles, whom Aeneas follows to the extent of sacrificing twelve prisoners of war. Up to this point the role of Achilles seemed to have devolved upon Turnus, the 'second Achilles' waiting in Latium referred to in the Sibyl's prophecy (VI 89–90, pp. 32–3): Turnus proudly refers to himself as an Achilles at IX 742. This role-change is significant of the Trojan revival and the inevitable defeat of Turnus. At the end of the poem, the sight of Pallas' baldric on Turnus gives Aeneas the same motive for killing Turnus that Achilles had for killing Hector: revenge. Aeneas is a complex character, *pius* but also a great soldier, perhaps Troy's greatest after Hector, and the motives of his final act are complex: revenge, dynastic necessity, and fate itself, which had narrowed the future down to this one significant moment, this one existential choice. Turnus would never have fitted into the coalition planned by Aeneas and Latinus; his pride, his egotism, his old-fashioned courage would all have got in the way of peace and progress. 'I shall introduce the gods of Troy to Italy', says Aeneas to Latinus in book XII, and his final killing of Turnus takes on something almost of the nature of a formal rite, even an *auto da fé*.

19 Fate and free will

The concept of fate (*fatum*) or destiny dominates the *Aeneid*. The word first occurs in the second line of the poem – *Italiam fato profugus Laviniaque venit/ ora* – in which *fato* must be taken both with *profugus* ('exiled by fate') and with *venit* ('came by fate to Italy'). The word occurs again, twice, soon after, in Jupiter's first speech to Venus in which he reassures the goddess that despite present adversities Aeneas will fulfil his destiny:

> manent immota tuorum
> *fata* tibi; cernes urbem et promissa Lavini
> moenia, sublimemque feres ad sidera caeli
> magnanimum Aenean; neque me sententia vertit. . .
> hic tibi (*fabor* enim, quando haec te cura remordet,
> longius, et volvens *fatorum* arcana movebo)   (I 257–262)
>> The destiny of your descendants
> Remains unchanged, you'll see the promised city walls
> And your great-hearted son you'll raise to heaven.
> Nothing has changed me, but since this worry eats at your heart
> I'll speak at greater length, and will unroll
> The secret book of fate.

fatum is connected with the verb *fari*, to speak: destiny is thus the expressed will of the gods. *fatum* also means the particular fate of individuals or nations: *fata tuorum* means the destiny of your race (the descendants of Aeneas). In the words of Jupiter quoted above, the metaphor changes from the spoken to the written word: Jupiter will unroll the book of destiny (for the form of the ancient book, see above, p. 36). All this suggests that fate is something predestined, known to the gods and to a few others gifted with prophetic powers, and unalterable. Some of the harshest words in the poem are spoken by the Sibyl to the shade of Palinurus, Aeneas' unburied helmsman, who begs Aeneas to take him across the river. Before Aeneas can speak, the Sibyl intervenes: *desine fata deum flecti sperare precando*: 'stop hoping that the will of the gods can be altered by prayer.' Seneca quotes these words with Stoic admiration in one of his letters and adds: 'all things are determined and fixed, and guided by everlasting Necessity.' It is a bleak philosophy, and the modern reader of the *Aeneid* may wonder how much room for manoeuvre is left to human free will.

In Homer divine intervention in human affairs by individual gods is direct, frequent and unpredictable; it cannot be dismissed as a series of metaphors for chance, though the existence of this pluralistic theocracy means that Homer did not need in addition the principle of chance which is virtually absent from his narrative: the gods decide all things. These manifestations are deeply confusing and distressing to the heroes, who have to operate with or against them as best they can. Ajax's great cry in *Iliad* XVII, 'If we must die, let us die in the light', is a reproach to Zeus for having cast a protective mist over the body of Patroclus. Athene tricks Hector in book XXII by disguising herself as his brother Deiphobus and then vanishing, so that Achilles can take Hector easily:

> Zeus puts out his golden scales
> and in them set two fateful portions of death,
> one for Achilles and one for Hector . . . and
>   Hector's death-day was heavier
> and dragged downwards towards death, and Phoebus
>   Apollo forsook him.

The gods desert their doomed champions. Zeus's action in putting out the scales does not mean he is questioning fate or trying to discover what it is, but is perhaps a symbolic demonstration of the destined outcome of an action about which, in the narrative, a moment of dramatic uncertainty is required.

Virgil does not wholly eliminate these divine interventions from his narrative; but he greatly reduces their frequency, and when they do occur they are treated seriously and imaginatively; the element of sheer frivolity and irresponsibility found in Homer's Olympians does not belong in Virgil's universal scheme of things. Juno's most notable attempt to rescue Turnus is allowed by Jupiter only on condition that the goddess clearly understands it can make no difference in the end (see above, pp. 91–2). And in the final encounter between Aeneas and Turnus, Jupiter sends a Fury which terrifies both Turnus himself and his sister Juturna, who is forced to abandon her brother as Apollo abandoned Hector. The Fury takes the form of an owl, the bird of ill-omen 'that sings late at night among tombs and on deserted roof-tops': the description of the bird's wings beating against Turnus' shield so that his flesh creeps is one of the most terrifying moments in the poem, an imaginative metaphor of the highest poetic order. The modern reader might perhaps compare a passage from

the end of Graham Greene's *Brighton Rock* in which Pinkie
drives to his final destruction: 'an enormous emotion beat on
him; it was like something trying to get in; the pressure of
gigantic wings against the glass.' Turnus' limbs turn to jelly,
he is like a man trying to run in a dream. That simile is
Homeric, but Virgil changes it significantly by saying 'when
in a dream *we* seem to run but falter', thereby allowing every
reader to identify with Turnus' final moments of isolation
and despair. Does he lose his free will in the face of divine
hostility, or is this a metaphor for the fear of death? The same
question might arise in the mind of the reader of Faustus' last
soliloquy in Marlowe's play: the problem is not peculiar to
paganism.

In the *Aeneid* the gods work *through* human wills and
desires: their interventions are often a metaphor for those
divine promptings, to good or ill, with which we are all
familiar. Mars in the *Aeneid* often simply means war, while
the visions of Venus vouchsafed to Aeneas are the very embodiment of peace, beauty and caring love. Yet the 'beguiling' of Vulcan by Venus in *Aeneid* VIII to persuade him to
make Aeneas' Shield is a piece of sexual anthropomorphism
straight out of Homer (the 'beguiling of Zeus' by Hera in
Iliad XIV). Jupiter is a more dignified version of Homer's
father Zeus; Homer seems to have envisaged the will of Zeus
as separate from, though co-ordinate with, destiny, and
destiny itself as the 'portion' allotted to each man at birth –
blessings, miseries, length of life – and lasting until the fates
finish spinning the thread of his life. Virgil, as we have seen,
regarded the will of Jupiter as the expression of fate, and fate
itself as more than the sum of individual destinies. Certain
events are predetermined, though the precise moment and circumstances of their fulfilment remains flexible, and this flexibility allows for the continued operation of human free will
and for the persistence of a pluralistic theocracy within the
larger philosophic framework which had evolved as concep-
tual thought became more sophisticated after Homer. We
know from Anchises' speech in book VI that Virgil sub-
scribed to the Stoic principle of rational determinism working

throughout the universe; *fatum* in the *Aeneid* is thus a sometimes confused amalgam of this universal principal, the irrational individualism of the Homeric system and a divine providence moving slowly and inevitably, albeit with many checks and reverses, towards justice and right.

The most striking instance in the *Aeneid* of human free will operating without divine interference occurs in book X, when Jupiter asserts his impartiality in the struggle between the Trojans and the Latins:

> Then, whatever each man's fortune is today, the hope each
>   pursues,
> Trojan or Rutulian, let him carve it out, I'll make no
>   distinction . . .
> Whatever each sets his hand to will bring him toil and fortune.
> King Jupiter is the same for all men,
> Fate will find the way.

Here the deity puts off the burden of responsibility for human fate, it becomes man's existential choice; on the plains of Latium man in his loneliness must enact history. The poet's use of his favourite narrative tense, the 'historic present', helps the reader to see this 'today' as any and every day, a paradigm of life as it must be lived through by us all. If the deity can suspend divine interference on one day, he can suspend it on any day. Men can no longer assume divine aid or divine hostility. They will find out soon enough whether their actions have won divine approval or provoked divine outrage.

20 Conclusions

Sainte-Beuve said of Virgil that he 'gave a new form to tastes, passions and sensibility', and that 'at a decisive moment of world history he foresaw what would appeal to the future'. The modern reader of the *Aeneid* is perhaps specially aware of the poem's power to generate alternative possibilities. If the *Iliad* 'celebrates the regularity and harmony of experience' (Silk, 102), the *Aeneid* explores its dislocations and dissonances: there is a sense as we read of the unrealised, of words not spoken, of things not enacted, of a world in which, perhaps, Aeneas stayed at Carthage, Evander did not lose his son, Turnus was spared, Marcellus survived to succeed Augustus.

It is a measure of the poem's modernity that it can be read in such different (and sometimes diametrically opposed) ways. The great passages of Augustan panegyric — Jupiter's and Anchises' prophesies, the presentation on Aeneas' Shield of the battle of Actium — are sometimes praised for the nobility and certainty with which they proclaim a new order, sometimes dismissed as propagandist, even fascist, though they are not greatly different, save in their artistic merit, from the jubilant rhetoric which attends the inauguration of new regimes even in democracies; and there can be little doubt that Virgil himself felt that 'bliss was it in that dawn to be alive', and, to start with at least, saw in Augustus the last, best hope of peace in Italy.

Yet much that the poem says seems to be suspended within the implied author's own doubts. The question 'do heavenly beings feel such anger?' (I 11) is a strange one for a poet to ask who has just embarked on a narrative motivated by the anger of Juno. And again, 'was it your will, Jupiter, that nations destined to eternal peace should clash in such a conflict?' (XII 503–4). Now Jupiter specifically stated (X 9) that the civil war between Trojans and Latins was in defiance of his ban (*contra vetitum discordia*), and Virgil is here evidently wrestling with the unanswerable question of how we reconcile evil with a rational cosmos.

Much of the poem's ambivalence comes from the poet's attitude to war. Homer took war for granted, for him it was a *donnée* of the heroic age. For Virgil Actium was a glorious victory against barbarism, with all the Olympian gods (at last) on the same side; yet the war Aeneas had to fight was a forbidden war, a war which divided and distressed the gods themselves: 'the gods in Jupiter's house feel pity for the useless anger of both sides and for all the great labours of men' (X 758–9). Do they? Or does the implied author bring that pity into his text? Is divine pity a transference of human? It is the reader who, through the intensity of Virgil's empathy, feels pity for Dido, for Evander, for Nisus and

Euryalus. Before Aeneas kills Lausus, one of those young untried warriors whose untimely deaths moved Virgil so deeply,
he speaks almost regretfully:

> Where are you rushing to, you who are doomed to die?
> Taking risks beyond your powers, your piety deceives you –
> (X 811–12)

and when Lausus dies Aeneas *thinks* of his own father and
holds out his hand in a gesture of pity. Yet what *verbal* con-
solation does he offer? Lausus will retain his armour and his
body be returned for burial – important considerations,
admittedly, in the heroic world – and he has been slain by
great Aeneas. Those last words are reminiscent of Homer's
self-vaunting Achilles, and this mixture of traditional heroic
behaviour and often unarticulated sensibility is one of the
hero's, and the poem's, most problematic traits.

One of the most poignant contrasts in the poem between
the achieved and the unachieved, the enacted and the sup-
pressed, occurs in a passage, itself remarkable, at the beginning of book VI: a passage which illustrates Virgil's power of
suggestive synthesis through a single polysemous visual sym-
bolism. Aeneas enters Apollo's temple at Cumae and sees
there sculptures of the Cretan labyrinth carved by its creator,
the master-craftsman Daedalus. He and his son Icarus were
forced to escape from Crete (using wings of his own invention); Icarus crashed and died, but Daedalus landed safely in
Italy. Here at Cumae, the entrance to the Virgilian underworld, he carved a representation of his famous maze. The
myth was well-known: Theseus penetrated the maze, killed
the monster at its centre, and escaped using a thread or clue
provided by the artificer himself. Theseus is not mentioned by
Virgil, but he could be an implied figure of Aeneas himself
and the labyrinth a figure of the underworld, especially as
Theseus' other exploits included a descent into Hades.
Daedalus, who fled with his son from a bronze-age city to
Italy, might also suggest Anchises and Aeneas, though in
their case it was the father who died, not the son.

Virgil ends his description by explaining the *absence* of any sculpture of Icarus: twice the father's hands essayed the work, twice they faltered. Emotion prevented articulation. Daedalus' grief for his son prefigures Evander's and Mezentius'. Is Daedalus also a figure of the poet himself, providing clues to his own secret creative processes? The line describing the maze, *hic labor ille domus et inextricabilis error* (VI 27), 'here the labour, here the house, and the irretraceable winding way', might stand both for Aeneas' journey into the underworld (*hoc opus, his labor est*, in the Sibyl's words, 'here the task, here the labour') and for the poet's own labours in constructing his intricate model of the house of the dead. It is surely significant that Virgil chose to place the myth of Daedalus at the very centre of his poem, at the very heart of his labyrinthine artefact. Characteristic, too, is the aposiopesis with which the poet breaks off and 'dissolves' the passage. Aeneas would have gone on looking at the sculptures had not the priestess arrived with fresh orders and the admonition: 'this is not the time to look at such displays'. This technique of 'fusing together the expressed and the suggested' (F. W. H. Myers, 1901) is not as all-pervasive as some romantic readings of the *Aeneid* have implied, but no reading of the poem can ignore it.

Chapter 4

The after-life of the *Aeneid*

21 Influence and reputation

Perhaps the most remarkable feature of the after-life of the *Aeneid* is the sheer variety of ways in which it has been read, explained, criticised, imitated and admired from late antiquity until our own time. Homer enjoyed no such continuity, for the study of Greek virtually disappeared from Europe in the Dark Ages and was not fully revived until the Renaissance. It is not possible here to consider in any detail the poem's role as a touchstone of changing literary taste or to enter the arid debate as to which was the greater, Homer or Virgil. Generally speaking, Homer was held to excel in invention or *ingenium*, Virgil in art, and the *Aeneid* was studied, copied and praised for its supreme technical mastery. Poetry was classified from antiquity to the Renaissance as a kind of rhetoric ('eloquent speech'), and almost every known rhetorical figure could be illustrated from the poem.

Virgil was always regarded as a learned poet, *doctus poeta*, and the *Aeneid* was seen as a treasure-house of ancient Italian lore, much of it preserved by Virgil from earlier Italian antiquaries. But the poem's chief claim to fame was its genre-status as the first great national epic to be written in imitation of Homer: as such it became itself the principal model for later poets striving to create national epics in their own vernaculars. The Troy legend which was Virgil's starting-point became popular in medieval and renaissance chivalric romance. In the early fifteenth century the Italian humanist poet Maffeo Vegio supplied a thirteenth book of the *Aeneid,* in which Aeneas' marriage to Lavinia was celebrated, and this addition found its way a century later into Gavin Douglas' 'thirteen books of the *Aeneid*', the first British translation of the poem.

The *Aeneid* was also admired because it was thought to have portrayed in the character of Aeneas a figure of the ideal prince or governor: this view finds eloquent expression in Sidney's *Apology for Poetry* and also in Dryden, whose preface to his classic English version emphasised the poem's moral and political aspects and assumed the function of epic to be 'to form the mind to heroic virtue by example'. In particular, a famous line in Anchises' speech to Aeneas in book VI about the Roman mission to rule the nations − 'to spare the defeated and war down the proud' − was praised by St Augustine in the *City of God*: the principle was a Roman political commonplace, yet it might seem to come close to Christian doctrine ('he hath put down the mighty from their seats').

It is in St Augustine, too, that we find one of the earliest testimonies to the poem's power to move the reader: in his *Confessions* 1.13 he tells how he wept for the death of Dido. Thus the poem could be read in many ways − as a superb piece of rhetoric, as a learned poem about primitive Italy and its legends, for its moral and political philosophy and for its powerful insights into human emotion. Finally, it enshrined for future generations living under less successful systems a vision of Roman imperialism at its noblest. Many of these aspects of the poem are brought together in Dante's *Divine Comedy*.

22 Virgil and Dante

The relationship of Virgil to Dante's *Divine Comedy* provides a unique case of loving homage by a later poet to an earlier. The *Divine Comedy* tells the story of one man's journey through hell and purgatory to Paradise. Part vision, part allegory, it is yet intensely realised, for the experiencing 'I'-figure is Dante himself − not Dante the author of the poem but Dante as his own epic hero. At the very start of this undertaking Dante protests his own inadequacy − 'I am not Aeneas, not Paul'. To guide him through hell and purgatory, and also to inspire him to record that journey, Dante arouses the shade of Virgil, dead for thirteen hundred years yet loved and revered by his Italian disciple as 'the glory and light of other poets'. Dante hails Virgil as his literary master; yet despite a number of references to and quotations from the *Aeneid* and the fourth eclogue (see above, p. 14), and despite Dante's professed admiration for Virgil's high style, his own poem is quite different in tone and structure, and Virgil's authority is not primarily stylistic but spiritual and intellectual.

Virgil leads Dante through hell and purgatory, drawing on his own poetry but extending his original insights to take account of Dante's own world-view: his discourse on love and free will in the central cantos of the *Purgatorio* is, as it were, Virgil updated by Dante. This projection of the pagan poet into an afterworld which contains all sinners, Christian as well as pagan, is done with great imaginative skill: thus, when the two poets encounter Ulysses, Virgil questions him in Greek, but when they meet Florentines whom Dante actually knew, Virgil stays outside the discourse. Much of Dante's hell is copied from Virgil – Charon, Cerberus, Minos, the souls waiting to cross the river; Dante even essays an imitation of Virgil's famous simile comparing the waiting souls to the falling leaves of autumn, though Virgil's second, and even more touching simile, of birds migrating to sunnier climes, is reduced by Dante to a single bird-call.

Virgil is generally said to represent for Dante the furthest limits to which rational humanism can reach without benefit of divine grace; yet Virgil is no pale allegory but a real character, and the relationship between the two poets is touchingly developed. At the end of the *Purgatorio* Virgil vanishes, for he can discern no further. At that moment Dante has been reunited with the shade of his great love Beatrice, who will guide him in Paradise. Delightedly, Dante turns to Virgil with an apposite quotation on his lips – 'I recognise the vestiges of an old desire [literally: an old flame]', the words of Dido about Aeneas (*Aen*. IV 23). But Virgil does not answer, for he has already departed, and Dante weeps, even in the presence of Beatrice, for his lost leader, somewhat as St Augustine had wept for Dido. It is a brilliant psychological stroke.

The importance for Dante of Virgil was not, however, solely his expertise in the hereafter. Although born under what he calls in the *Inferno* 'the false and lying gods', he also lived 'under the good Augustus'. For Dante the emperor represented the providential inauguration of the Roman empire, and the *Pax Augusta* prepared the world for the birth of Christ. Despairing of the medieval conflict between the papacy and the Holy Roman Empire, Dante hoped that with the accession of a new emperor the golden age prophesied by Virgil would return and imperial Rome would be sanctified. The coming of the Trojan Aeneas to Italy was seen by Dante as the first stage in a divine plan which would lead to 'the salvation of that humble Italy for which Camilla, Nisus, Euryalus and Turnus died' (*Inferno* 1. 106–8).

It is sometimes wondered why Dante chose to leave Virgil in Limbo, home of the virtuous pagans (itself modelled on Virgil's Elysium), while yet placing Cato (whom Virgil in *Aeneid* VIII 670 gave jurisdiction over the souls of the righteous) in Purgatory and – more astonishingly – Rhipeus, mentioned at *Aen*. II 426 as 'the most just of the Trojans', in Paradise. Dante may have intended to show that, while nothing is beyond the power and love of God, nevertheless Virgil's peculiar significance lay in his imprisonment in that classical civilisation of which he is the supreme embodiment. For Dante Virgil remains on the very threshold of Christian enlightenment, 'dreaming in Parnassus of the earthly Paradise' (*Purgatorio* 28. 141), and is likened (*Purgatorio* 22. 67–72) to a man carrying a lantern, himself walking in darkness yet showing the way to those who come after. From his prolonged intercourse with Virgil's shade Dante drew the spiritual and intellectual strength necessary for him to understand and transcribe the ultimate mysteries of Paradise.

23 Virgil and renaissance epic

During the sixteenth century several European poets composed epics in their own vernaculars – Camoens' *Lusiads* about Vasco da Gama, Tasso's *Gerusalemme Liberata* about the Crusades, Ariosto's *Orlando Furioso* about Roland. All were inspired by Virgil to glorify the exploits and lineage of real or legendary national heroes. In England, Spenser's *Faerie Queene* offered a multiplicity of heroes whose exploits are often romantic, even erotic. But Spenser imitated Virgil's praise of Augustus as the descendant of the Trojan Aeneas by employing a fanciful genealogy taken from medieval British chroniclers, in which the British royal line was implausibly derived from a Trojan called Brutus. He chose as his principal characters Arthur, legendary champion of British independence, and a warrior-maid called Britomart who resembles Virgil's Camilla and represents one facet of Elizabeth I, to whom, as empress as well as queen, the poem is dedicated. Spenser's quaintly archaic style is far removed from Virgil's mature and sophisticated discourse; nevertheless Spenser consciously saw himself as the English Virgil, beginning his literary career with pastorals and ending with epic, as Virgil had done.

Spenser's variety of heroes and stories is also far removed from Virgil's single-minded concentration on a single hero (*'arms and the man* I sing . . .'). This single-mindedness did not find expression again until Milton's *Paradise Lost*, the greatest English epic and the only poem inspired by the *Aeneid* which successfully transposes both the theme and the structure of its model into its own discourse. Instead of the stream of rhyming stanzas which make up the cantos of Spenser or Tasso, Milton chose blank verse as the nearest equivalent to the unrhymed classical hexameter, dividing his text into twelve books. He also used Virgil's synchronism, so that his hero Adam prefigures Christ (the second Adam) as Aeneas prefigured Augustus. And just as the expulsion and exile of Aeneas from Troy (by a trick, the wooden horse) was a necessary prelude to the rise of Rome, so the expulsion and exile of Adam and Eve from Eden (through the trick of the apple) was the necessary prelude in the divine plan to the Incarnation and eventual second coming of Christ.

Milton's teleological epic of Christian heroism transcends its pagan model. When Michael in *P.L.* 12 foretells to Adam that Christ

> shall ascend
> The throne hereditary, and bound his reign
> With earth's wide bounds, his glory with the heavens

the words are an allusion both to Jupiter's prophesy in *Aeneid* I 287 about Augustus and Anchises' prophesy to Aeneas in book VI 782: Jupiter foretells that Augustus

> imperium Oceano, famam qui terminet astris
> will bound his empire with Ocean, his fame with the stars;

Anchises foretells that Rome

> imperium terris, animos aequabit Olympo
> will measure her empire with the world, her spirit with heaven.

The Virgilian concept of empire without end is thus reaffirmed by Milton in an all-embracing Christian reading of universal history. Milton takes to its furthest possible limits the renaissance idea that the most valuable pagan texts were those which could be read as allegories of divine truth; these take on a kind of 'meta-significance' to which their original authors could have had no access.

Milton drew heavily on the cosmological didacticism of the *Aeneid*. Just as Aeneas was introduced in future and past events by the Sibyl, Anchises and Evander, so Milton's Adam is instructed by the angels, Raphael and Michael about the origins of Satan's fall from heaven, the creation of man and the whole of the future from the Incarnation to the second coming and the final dissolution of the created world, an apocalyptic vision again based on Virgil:

> New heaven and earth, wherein the just shall dwell,
> And after all their tribulations long
> See golden days, fruitful of golden deeds.

So too Anchises foretells to Aeneas that Augustus will bring back the golden age to Italy.

Into the character of Adam, his often-doubting hero, Milton put something of Aeneas; into the mighty figure of Satan, his anti-hero, he put something of Turnus and something too of Juno: Satan's 'sense of injured merit' (a reference to God's exaltation of the Messiah over the other angels) is a clear reference to Juno's *spretae . . . iniuria formae*, the 'injury done to her spurned beauty'. But whereas Virgil's Juno is reconciled to Rome, Milton's Satan cannot be reconciled to God.

23 Virgil and romanticism

During the eighteenth century there was a revival of interest in Homer as a 'child of nature' whose poetry portrays unself-consciously the very dawn of civilisation: a revival partly, and rather oddly, sparked off by Pope's *Iliad*, a version far more Augustan than Homeric. But if Virgil's sophistication and polish seemed studied and alien to the romantics with their emphasis on spontaneity, his profound feeling for human passions, doubt and despair struck a chord in the sensibility of the nineteenth century. Berlioz's opera *The Trojans* (1856–8), based on *Aeneid* II and IV, is the supreme artistic expression of a romanticised Virgil. Berlioz had two literary idols, Virgil and Shakespeare, and in the love-duet of Dido and Aeneas he combined the two, drawing on the love-scene between Lorenzo and Jessica in *The Merchant of Venice*, 5.1, in which Shakespeare himself refers to Dido:

> In such a night
> Stood Dido with a willow in her hand
> Upon the wild sea-banks, and waft her love
> To come again to Carthage.

Berlioz saw the *Aeneid* in typically nineteenth-century terms as a dialectic between love and history. At about the same time (1857) Sainte-Beuve published his seminal lectures on Virgil, drawing fresh attention to the poet's great powers of empathy with the human condition. Some modern writers have tended to emphasise Aeneas' doubts and dilemmas about his heroic mission and to identify these as Virgil's own: this autobiographical reading of the *Aeneid* finds its most extreme expression in Hermann Broch's novel *Virgil's Death* (*Der Tod des Vergil*, 1945), which, taking as its starting-point the tradition in the ancient life that the poet wanted the manuscript of his epic destroyed, analyses at great length the poet's dying reservations about his achievement and that of Augustus. We have come a long way from Jupiter's great vision of *imperium sine fine*, empire without end.

Principal characters of the poem

(No book-reference is given against the names of characters who appear throughout the poem)

Achilles	Principal Greek hero of Homer's *Iliad*
Aeneas	eponymous hero of the *Aeneid* (Homer's Aineias), son of Anchises and Venus
Aeolus	minor deity in charge of the winds (I)
Allecto	one of the Furies, sent by Juno to arouse Turnus against Aeneas (VII)
Amata	wife of King Latinus
Anchises	father of Aeneas
Antony (Marcus Antonius)	Roman leader defeated by Augustus (VIII)
Apollo	one of the principal deities of the Graeco-Roman pantheon, pro-Trojan in Homer and Virgil; tutelary deity of Augustus
Ascanius	Aeneas' son by his wife Creusa
Atlas	deity who bears the universe on his shoulders
Augustus Caesar (Octavian)	ruler of the Roman world (*princeps*) from 31 BC to AD 14
Cacus	fire-breathing monster killed by Hercules on the Aventine hill on the site of Rome (VIII)
Camilla	warrior-maid, queen of the Volsci, protégée of Diana (VII, XI)
Charon	ferryman of the dead across the river of the underworld (VI)
Cleopatra	queen of Egypt, ally of Mark Antony (VIII)
Creusa	wife of Aeneas (II)

Diana	(the Greek Artemis) goddess of virginity
Dido	queen of Carthage, lover of Aeneas
Diomedes	Greek hero in Homer's *Iliad*, who settled in Italy after the Trojan war
Drances	Italian leader who opposes Turnus out of personal hatred (XI)
Euryalus	a young Trojan hero (IX)
Evander	Arcadian immigrant settled at Pallanteum on the site of Rome (VIII)
Hector	principal Trojan hero in Homer's *Iliad*, killed by Achilles (II)
Hercules	(Greek Heracles) a hero famous for his labours, later deified
Iarbas	suitor to Dido (IV)
Juno	(Homer's Hera), anti-Trojan in both Homer and Virgil
Jupiter	king of the gods (Homer's Zeus)
Juturna	a nymph, sister of Turnus (XII)
Laocoon	Trojan priest, who suspects the stratagem of the wooden horse but is unable to convince his countryman (II)
Latinus	Italian ruler, king of the Laurentes, who offers the Trojans an alliance
Lausus	son of Mezentius, killed by Aeneas (X)
Lavinia	daughter of Latinus, betrothed to Turnus but destined to marry Aeneas
Mars	god of war (the Greek Ares)
Mercury	messenger of the gods (the Greek Hermes)
Mezentius	Etruscan renegade, killed by Aeneas (X)
Neptune	god of the sea (Greek Poseidon)
Nisus	young Trojan hero, friend of Euryalus (IX)
Octavian	see Augustus

Pallas	(1) the goddess Minerva (the Greek Athene)
	(2) son of Evander, killed by Turnus
Paris	Trojan hero, 'husband' of Helen in Homer's *Iliad*
Phoebus	Apollo
Priam	king of Troy, killed by Achilles' son Pyrrhus (II)
Romulus	traditional founder of Rome, subsequently deified as Quirinus
Saturn	ancient Roman deity, identified with the Greek Cronos, father of Jupiter (Zeus), who was expelled by his son from Olympus and took refuge in Latium where he presided over a 'golden age' (VIII)
Sychaeus	late husband of Dido
Tarchon	Etruscan king, allied to Aeneas
Turnus	Italian leader, king of the Rutuli, principal foe and rival of Aeneas
Venus	(Greek goddess Aphrodite), mother of Aeneas
Ulysses	(Homer's Odysseus), perpetrator of the stratagem of the wooden horse.

Guide to further reading

(a) Editions, commentaries, translations

The standard Latin edition (without commentary) is edited by R. A. B. Mynors (Oxford Classical Texts, second edn. 1972). A text with facing English translation is in the Loeb series, by H. R. Fairclough (London and Cambridge, Mass. 1934–5). The most useful Latin text with commentary is edited by R. D. Williams (2 vols., London, 1972–3). Its predecessor in the same Macmillan series, edited by T. E. Page, (London, 1894–1900) remains valuable. Editions of individual books of the *Aeneid* are mainly for the specialist, but R. G. Austin's editions of books, I, II, IV, and VI (Oxford, 1971, 1973, 1963, 1986) constitute a major contribution to our understanding of the poem. K. W. Gransden's edition of book VIII (Cambridge, 1976) includes a substantial introductory essay on the poem as a whole. Among older commentaries, W. Warde Fowler's *Virgil's Gathering of the Clans* (Oxford, 1916), *Aeneas at the Site of Rome* (Oxford, 1917) and *The Death of Turnus* (Oxford, 1919) consist of texts, facing translations and expositions of key passages in books VII, VIII and XII: their scholarship has been to some extent superseded but they remain valuable examples of humane learning.

Of the translations referred to in this book, Dryden's classic version (1697) has been frequently reprinted, e.g. in the World's Classics series (Oxford, 1961) and most recently in 1986 (Bristol, Classical Press). Also recommended are the versions by A. Mandelbaum (New York, 1961), C. Day Lewis (repr. Oxford, 1986) and R. Fitzgerald (Penguin, 1985).

The ancient *Life* of Virgil by Aelius Donatus referred to in ch. 1.2 is translated as Appendix 1 of W. A. Camps' book listed under (c) below. R. G. Coleman's edition of the *Eclogues*, referred to in ch.1.3, is in the Cambridge Greek and Latin classics series (1977) and contains an important introduction.

(b) Background

On the historical background of the poem and Virgil's life, the most important book remains R. Syme's *The Roman Revolution* (Oxford, 1939). See also W. Tarn and M. P. Charlesworth, *Octavian, Antony and Cleopatra* (repr. from the *Cambridge Ancient History*, vol. x, chs. 1–4, 1965). On the legend of Aeneas see G. K. Galinsky, *Aeneas, Sicily and Rome* (Princeton, 1969). On ancient Italy see R. M. Ogilvie, *Early Rome and the Etruscans* (London, 1976) and A. G. Mackay, *Vergil's Italy* (New York, 1971). On Roman mythology and religion see M. Grant, *Roman Myths* (London, 1971) and R. M. Ogilvie, *The Romans and their Gods* (London, 1969).

On the Homeric background see the *Landmarks* books by M. Silk on *The Iliad* and J. Griffin on *The Odyssey* (both Cambridge, 1987). G. Knauer's *Die Aeneis und Homer* (Göttingen, 1964) is a seminal work of reference giving a line-by-line listing of every Virgilian allusion to Homer. On the *Aeneid* as a landmark in the evolution of the epic see J. K. Newman, *The Classical Epic Tradition* (Wisconsin, 1986).

(c) Literary interpretations

The most important book on the *Aeneid* as epic narrative remains R. Heinze's *Vergils epische Technik* (repr. Stuttgart, 1965): an English translation is in preparation. Meanwhile, the most accessible mediator of Heinze is Brooks Otis, *Virgil: A Study in Civilised Poetry* (Oxford, 1963). More recent general surveys of the poem are by W. A. Camps, *Virgil's Aeneid: a Critical Introduction* (Oxford, repr. 1986); K. Quinn, *Virgil's Aeneid: A Critical Description* (London,

1968), and R. D. Williams, *The Aeneid* (London, 1987); the book by Camps is particularly helpful.

More specialised, but still accessible, studies include V. Pöschl, *The Art of Virgil: Image and Symbol in the Aeneid*, English translation by G. Seligson (Ann Arbor, 1962); W. R. Johnson, *Darkness Visible* (California, 1976), a highly original if sometimes eccentric study of the poem's psychological and spiritual implications; K. W. Gransden, *Virgil's Iliad: an Essay on Epic Narrative* (Cambridge, 1984), which deals chiefly with the second half of the poem. Primarily for the specialist, but offering important insights into analogies between the political world of the poem and the physical universe, is P. Hardie, *Virgil's Aeneid: Cosmos and Imperium* (Oxford, 1986).

Finally, three earlier works mentioned in this book: Sainte-Beuve, *Etude sur Virgile* (Paris, 1857) has some claim to be the first modern approach to the poem by a major critic; F. W. H. Myers's 'Virgil' in his *Essays Classical* (London, 1901), though tinged with Arnoldian romanticism, offers some far-seeing comments on how the poetry works; T. S. Eliot's *What is a Classic*? (an address delivered to the Virgil Society, London, 1944) authoritatively asserts the poem's central place in European culture.

(d) After-life

The standard work on post-Virgilian epic remains C. M. Bowra, *From Virgil to Milton* (London, 1945). The book by J. K. Newman listed under (b) surveys the classical epic tradition from Homer to the twentieth century. A useful general essay on the poem's influence is included in the book by R. D. Williams listed under (c), ch. 8. See also the same author's 'Changing Attitudes to Virgil' in *Studies in Latin Literature and its Influence: Virgil*, ed. D. R. Dudley (London, 1969), which also contains useful contributions by A. G. Mackay on 'Virgil and Landscape' (with reproductions of paintings by Claude, Turner, etc.) and J. H. Whitfield on 'Virgil into Dante'. Other recent relevant essays on Dante are by

R. Kirkpatrick in the *Landmarks* series (Cambridge 1987) (ch. 1), and P. Armour, 'Dante's Virgil', in *Virgil in a cultural tradition*, ed. R. A. Caldwell and J. Hamilton (Nottingham, 1986). On Virgil and Milton see K. W. Gransden, 'The Aeneid and Paradise Lost' in *Virgil and his Influence*, ed. C. Martindale (Bristol, 1984). These two collections of essays are among a number of books published to mark the bimillenium of Virgil's birth; they contain a variety of contributions on many aspects of the poet's achievement and influence.